Rubens to Rhubarb

The Ringling Museum Cookbook

Presented by

The John and Mable Ringling Museum of Art

The State Art Museum of Florida

Rubens to Rhubarb

The Ringling Museum Cookbook

THE JOHN AND MABLE RINGLING MUSEUM OF ART
The State Art Museum of Florida
5401 Bay Shore Road
Sarasota, Florida 34243

Publisher
Constance L. Holcomb

Production Editor & Compositor
Anne M. Parker, Associate Professor
Manatee Community College

Recipes
Helen L. Lawson

Historical notes
David C. Weeks

Editorial & Marketing Consultant
Gayle Hanley Levy

Design Consultant
Bryan Winke Design

Cover concept
Robert S. McComb

Title
Walter D. Serwatka

Grateful acknowledgment is made to University Press of Florida for permission to use material from *Ringling: the Florida Years, 1911-1936*, by David C. Weeks © 1993 University Press of Florida.

ISBN 0-916758-35-4. Library of Congress Catalog Number 95-077893. Second printing.

Copyright acknowledgments, cover and photo identification follow page 237.

Table of Contents

Introduction

I am pleased to introduce *Rubens to Rhubarb*, a unique cookbook published by The John and Mable Ringling Museum of Art Foundation. The recipes have been selected to appeal to a broad range of tastes and may be used in a variety of menus. We anticipate that you will find equal pleasure in the color photographs and historical notes detailing the lives of John and Mable Ringling and the delights that await thousands of people who visit the Museum each year.

The John and Mable Ringling Museum of Art, created in the 1920s, still reflects the image and character of its period and its founders. John, one of the famous Ringling brothers, and his wife, Mable, built a magnificent Venetian-style winter home on the Sarasota Bay, at the height of the Florida real estate boom. They named it Cà d'Zan, meaning House of John in Venetian dialect. Nearby they built their art museum, modeled on an Italian Renaissance villa, in which they housed a formidable and growing art collection.

By 1931, when financial difficulties put an end to his collecting, John Ringling had acquired over 600 paintings, including works by Peter Paul Rubens and other masters of Italian and Flemish 17th-century art. Among other treasures were the Cesnola Collection of Cypriot Antiquities and Emile Gavet's 19th-century collection of European decorative arts. Upon John's death in 1936, the art museum, the Cà d'Zan and its surrounding acres of tropical gardens were bequeathed to the people of Florida to be known in perpetuity as The John and Mable Ringling Museum of Art.

In over half a century since the State of Florida assumed ownership in 1946, the Museum has grown to become one of the top 30 museums in the United States, welcoming more than 270,000 visitors each year. The Museum now holds over 10,000 works of art, including many prints and drawings, a modern art collection, innumerable circus artifacts in its Circus Museum, a library with over 55,000 volumes and extensive archives. In 1950, a 19th-century theater was acquired from Asolo, Italy, and re-sited on the Museum grounds. The Asolo Theater became the initial home to a wide variety of performing arts groups which, with The John and Mable Ringling Museum of Art, give Sarasota its cultural preeminence in Florida today.

Enjoy *Rubens to Rhubarb* and feast with us on the legacy of an extraordinary individual: John Ringling, circus showman, financier, real estate developer, oil and railroad entrepreneur, art collector and founder of one of America's great museums.

David Ebitz
Director

A Tribute to Helen L. Lawson

When Helen Lawson, author of the recipes in *Rubens to Rhubarb*, was asked about her favorite part of The John and Mable Ringling Museum of Art, she said, "I love the big kitchen in the Cà d'Zan. . . . Oh, and I would like their staff, too." Then, smiling at her attorney husband, Rod, she quickly added, "He's my staff, though."

Although Longboat Key, Florida, has been Rod and Helen Lawson's winter residence for almost thirty years, their family home is Stillwater, Minnesota. It was there they raised three accomplished children and watched their four grandchildren grow up.

The recipes in this cookbook began with the heritage of Helen Lawson's family. Her wish to pass along her grandmother's, mother's and her own recipes to her children resulted in the publication and success of her first book, *Helen Lawson's Heritage Cookbook*, now in its fourth printing. Over the years Helen has continued to collect recipes and to expand that first volume into this collection, a tribute to her ancestors, which she has now generously donated to The John and Mable Ringling Museum of Art.

Heritage and history are a very significant part of the Lawsons' lives. In the early 1970s Rod started the momentum for the restoration of their hometown of Stillwater, Minnesota, the booming turn-of-the-century hub of the lumber industry. Today, Helen, a University of Minnesota graduate, regularly attends a bimonthly "Friday Study Group" founded by her mother and several friends in 1924 to stimulate intellectual interests for women. Helen's participation in the Stillwater Historical Society led her to discover that John Ringling's father briefly owned a harness-making business on Main Street in Stillwater in the 1800s.

In addition to her interests in history, Helen has chaired the Hospital Auxiliary Board, served on the Stillwater Library Board for 20 years, participates in the local branch of the American Association of University Women and regularly plays golf and tennis. And, not surprisingly, she loves to cook.

John and Mable Ringling enjoyed rather simple and sometimes hearty fare prepared for them by their long time cook and friend. Helen Lawson's philosophy parallels the Ringlings' taste, and she says, "I love to cook but would not call myself a gourmet cook. I can do recipes that are hard, but I feel good things don't have to be fancy."

Explaining her motivation for handing down her family's recipes, Helen commented, "Only if your motives are for progeny, not for profit, should you proceed." The John and Mable Ringling Museum of Art, a gift from the Ringlings to the State of Florida, now enjoys a gift from Helen Lawson to help sustain it.

Foreword

When my husband, Wally, and I moved to Florida's west coast a couple of years ago, we quickly learned that Sarasota was widely considered the cultural center of Florida. Indeed, we soon discovered its theater, opera and ballet companies, performing arts centers, galleries, and a renowned art and design school. And, at the heart of this community, we discovered the extraordinary cultural treasure which in many ways defines Sarasota, The John and Mable Ringling Museum of Art.

As the State Art Museum of Florida, about thirty percent of its operating budget comes from the state. Therefore, contributions are essential for restorations, upkeep and many of its special programs. With a background in publishing and a desire to contribute, the idea of a Museum publication sprang to mind. A book with favorite recipes, color photographs and interesting historical notes seemed a good way to introduce many people to the Ringlings and the Museum, while at the same time raising funds for its preservation and support.

Those who have experienced the classic grandeur of this Museum, with its extraordinary collections, magnificent Ringling mansion, memorable Circus Museum and charming Asolo Theater understand the motivation I feel to preserve and promote this gem. If you are an old friend to the Museum, as I now feel I am, I hope you will be moved to return and savor again the pleasures that await within. If you are as yet unfamiliar with this treasure, I hope that *Rubens to Rhubarb* will be your invitation to come and explore the Ringling legacy to the people of Florida.

I wish to express my appreciation to Helen Lawson for giving us her family recipes and to David Weeks for his significant contribution of the historical notes. Many thanks to the dedicated people who cheerfully wrote, cooked, read, edited, designed, critiqued, typed and retyped the endless changes made to this work. I have listed their names and contributions on the following page. I am also grateful to the Volunteer Center of Sarasota for introducing me to so many talented and interesting people without whom this project would not have been possible.

Constance L. Holcomb
Publisher

Special Thanks

A special note of thanks to all who contributed their skill, time, energy and enthusiasm to the development and sale of this cookbook.

Recipe Author
Helen L. Lawson

Recipe Editorial Board
Trish Brown
Virginia C. Bryan
Roderick Lawson
James Moser
Ruth Moser
Ann F. Noll
Anne M. Parker
Gerda Schaefer
Robin Solomon
Lydia E. Towner
Beverly T. Vernon
Pamela Wall
Charlotte Woznicki
Elinor Zuch

Recipe Testing Cooks
Jean Speed
Mary Ann Stevens

Menus
Virginia C. Bryan
Beverly T. Vernon

Historical Notes Author
David C. Weeks

Editorial Consultant
Gayle Hanley Levy

Copy Editors
Ellen Eastwood
Walter D. Serwatka

Page Design & Typography
Anne M. Parker

Cover Design & Graphics
Robert S. McComb
Bryan Winke Design

Art & Photography Coordination
Robert S. McComb

Color Separations
Klay Printing, Tampa, FL

Title
Walter D. Serwatka

Promotion & Direct Marketing
Gayle Hanley Levy
Caryl Lambert
Bonnie LoFrumento
Vidisha A. Patel
Denise Rieth

Account Development & Sales
Trish Brown
Caryl Lambert
Warren B. Russell
Robert S. McComb
Virginia C. Bryan

Press Relations
Robin Solomon
Beverly T. Vernon

Museum Advisers
John H. Evans
Mary C. Geldi
Barbara Kate Linick
Mark Ormond
Jocelyn U. Stevens

John Nicholas Ringling (1866 - 1936).

Mable Burton Ringling (1875 - 1929).

Menus

Ladies' Luncheon

Black Tie Blinis with Caviar*
Asheville Salad*
Everglades Asparagus Vinaigrette*
Daytona Date Nut Bread*
Florida Key Lime Pie*

Sparkling White Wine
Sparkling Iced Mineral Water with Lemon Slice

Holiday Cocktail Party

Spanikopitas*
Swedish Meatballs*
Brie Baked en Croûte* with Apple & Pear Slices
St. Petersburg Caviar Pie*
Asparagus Wrapped with Smoked Salmon*
Golden Gate Point Blue Cheese Spread*
Assorted Crackers, Melba Toast & French Bread Slices

Soft Drinks - Mixed Drinks - Beer
Chenin Blanc

An Elegant Dinner

Corey's Landing Crabmeat Cocktail*
St. Croix Liver Pâté* with Toast Points
Beef Stroganoff* with Buttered Egg Noodles
Sherried Broiled Tomatoes*
Dinner Rolls*
Grand Marnier Strawberry Ice*
Aunt Ruth's Lace Cookies*

Sparkling Mineral Water
Muscadet or Sauvignon Blanc
Merlot
Coffee - Tea

* Recipe is in this book. Please refer to the index.

Champagne Brunch Buffet

Suncoast Broiled Grapefruit*
South Florida Hot Chicken Salad*
Savory Beef Brisket*
Symphony Spinach Strawberry Salad*
Big Pass Blueberry Muffins*
Crème de Menthe Chocolate Bars*
Luscious Lemon Bars*
Lido Casino Candied Nuts*

Champagne - Mimosas
Coffee - Tea - Sparkling Water

Florida Beach Picnic

Countrytime Spareribs*
Dade County Deviled Eggs*
Boston Baked Beans*
Mangrove Island Marinated Cucumbers*
Coral Gables Garden Potato Salad*
Southern Cornbread*
Punta Gorda Peanut Butter Cookies*
Wally's Oatmeal Cookies*

Lemonade -- Beer - Soft Drinks

Sunday Night Supper

Marco Island Fresh Mushroom Soup*
Mandarin Chicken Salad with Melon*
Zesty Marinated Carrot Sticks*
Royal Palm Rhubarb Pie*

Soft Drinks - Iced Tea
Coffee

Menus

Pasta Party
Antipasto Primavera*
Linguine with Palms Elysian Pesto Sauce*
Spaghetti with Italian Spaghetti Sauce*
Italian Garlic Bread
Tableside Caesar Salad*
Tallahassee Macaroon Biscuit Tortoni*

Chianti
Beer - Coffee - Tea

Florida Sunset Buffet
Hot Cheese & Mustard Canapes*
Bacon-Wrapped Water Chestnuts*
Coquina Chicken with Crabmeat*
Masterpiece Marinated Pork Roast*
Creamy Broccoli Ring*
Hillsborough Browned Rice*
Florida Tomatoes with Red Wine Vinaigrette*
Dinner Rolls*
Clown Alley Cheese Cake*
Chocolate-Dipped Strawberries*

Sauvignon Blanc - Pinot Noir
Port or Sherry with Dessert
Coffee - Tea

Stay-Trim Menu
Broiled Marinated Swordfish with Angel Hair Pasta*
Asparagus Grapefruit Salad*
Italian Bread Sticks
Lightning Lemon Ice*

Iced Tea - Iced Coffee
Sparkling Mineral Water

Tail Gate Party

Bengal Cream Cheese Spread*
Hurricane Horseradish Dip*
Assorted Crackers and Chips
Hearty Lasagna*
Italian Bread Slices
Sliced Fresh Fruit with Sweet Fruit Dressing*
Gulf Stream Spinach Salad*
Tampa Bay Brownies*

Bloody Marys - Beer - Red Wine
Coffee - Soft Drinks

After Theater Sweet Table for 25

Brandy Alexander Pie*
French Silk Pie*
Lauderdale Lemon Meringue Pie*
Georgia Pecan Pie*
Big Top Chocolate Cake*
Arcadia Carrot Nut Cake*
Sunset Lime Soufflé*
Tidy Island Toffee Nut Bars*
Decadent Chocolate Fudge*
Alpine White Chocolate Truffles*
Magic Mixed Nut Bars*

Port - Champagne
Espresso - Cappuccino

Informal Family Dinner

Opera House Baked Chicken in Sherry Sauce*
Fluffy Buttered White Rice
Tossed Green Salad
Festive French Dressing*
Phillippi Creek Italian Zucchini*
Mother's Apple Crisp*
Tea - Coffee - Soft Drinks

Appetizers & Dips

Black Tie Blinis with Caviar

Preparation time: 30 minutes
Cooking time: 20 minutes

Makes 8 blinis

3	large eggs, separated
¼	cup flour
¼	cup milk
1	teaspoon grated orange peel
½	teaspoon salt
⅛	teaspoon pepper
4	ounces black caviar
1	cup sour cream (optional)
¼	cup red onion, chopped (optional)
1	lemon, cut into wedges (optional)

In medium bowl, with electric mixer, beat egg yolks, slowly adding flour and salt to blend. With mixer on medium-low, gradually add orange peel, pepper and milk.

In separate bowl, beat egg whites until stiff. Gently fold into yolk mixture.

Heat a non-stick 6" skillet over low heat. Pour a scant ¼ cup batter, tilting pan to spread batter evenly. Cook about 30 seconds, or when edges begin to look dry but center is still slightly wet. Lightly cook other side, about 10 - 15 seconds. Remove from skillet.

Continue cooking until all batter is used. Stack cooked blinis between sheets of waxed paper.

To assemble, spread each blini with about ½ tablespoon caviar. Roll and place seam side down. Arrange on serving platter. Top each blini with a dollop of sour cream.

Try this substitution: combine ¼ pound coarsely diced smoked salmon with 1 cup sour cream. Fill each blini, roll and serve. These need no topping.

Brie Baked en Croûte

Preparation time: 40 minutes
Cooking time: 20 minutes

Serves 12

1	sheet frozen puff pastry
1	pound Brie cheese
¼	cup sliced toasted almonds
⅓	cup chopped parsley
1	egg beaten with 1 teaspoon water

Preheat oven according to puff pastry instructions.

Thaw frozen puff pastry 25 minutes. On a floured surface, roll pastry into a 14" circle. Slice Brie in half horizontally, sprinkle bottom half with almonds and parsley. Cover with top half. Place in center of pastry circle. Brush pastry edges with beaten egg. Wrap Brie in pastry. Place Brie seam side down on an ungreased baking sheet. Brush with remaining egg wash. Bake 20 minutes. Let stand for 12 minutes before serving with crackers or fruit.

Captiva Cheddar Cheese Ball

Preparation time: 20 minutes

Makes 1 cheese ball

1	3-ounce package cream cheese, softened
½	pound sharp cheddar, grated
4	ounces blue cheese, crumbled
3	tablespoons brandy
1	green onion, minced
1	teaspoon paprika
½	cup chopped nuts

In mixing bowl, combine cheeses, brandy and onion. Beat on medium speed with electric mixer until well blended. Cover and refrigerate 1 hour.

Remove and shape into ball. Dust with paprika. Roll in nuts. Serve with assorted crackers. This can be made 1 - 2 days ahead, wrapped well and refrigerated.

St. Petersburg Caviar Pie

Preparation time: 30 minutes
Chilling time: 4 hours

Serves 8 - 10

5	hard boiled eggs, chopped
1	medium onion, finely chopped
3	tablespoons butter, melted
2	tablespoons margarine, melted
½	cup sour cream
1	3½ - 4 ounce jar red or black caviar
1	lemon thinly sliced
	parsley for garnish

Line a 7" or 8" round shallow dish with plastic wrap, allowing edges to overhang.

Add chopped eggs and onion to melted butter and margarine and mix well. Season with pepper. Pat mixture in prepared dish and chill at least 4 hours.

When ready to serve, turn dish onto serving platter. Remove plastic wrap. Frost top and sides with sour cream. Spread caviar over all. Garnish platter with lemon slices and parsley. Serve with Melba toast.

Over 500 years of European and American art are represented in The John and Mable Ringling Museum of Art, including one of the nation's most important collections of 16th- and 17th-century Italian and Flemish baroque paintings. At the core of this remarkable collection are a total of eight monumental works by Peter Paul Rubens.

The work of many other artists is represented as well, including the Italians Bassano, di Cosimo, Panini, Tintoretto and Veronese; the French Poussin and Boudin; the Spanish El Greco and Velázquez; the Dutch Hals and de Heem; and the English Reynolds and Gainsborough.

Hot Olive Cheese Puffs

Preparation time: 20 minutes
Cooking time: 15 minutes

Makes 48

2	cups grated sharp cheddar cheese
½	cup butter or margarine, softened
1	cup flour
½	teaspoon salt
1	teaspoon paprika
48	small stuffed green olives

Preheat oven to 400°.

With electric mixer blend cheese and margarine. With mixer on low, gradually add flour, salt and paprika. Mix just to blend. Chill dough for 1 hour. Pinch off a small amount of dough (about the size of a walnut) roll into ball, then flatten to small disk. Wrap around each olive. Pinch to seal. Place on ungreased baking. Bake 15 minutes. Serve warm.

Hot Cheese & Mustard Canapés

Preparation time: 30 minutes
Cooking time: 7 minutes

Makes 48

10	ounces sharp cheddar cheese, grated
1	8-ounce package cream cheese, softened
1	medium onion, minced
2	tablespoons each Red Raspberry mustard, Worcestershire sauce
1	cup mayonnaise
1	loaf French baguette, sliced ¼" thick

Preheat broiler.

On baking sheet, toast bread slices on one side. Mix first 6 ingredients together until well blended. Spread 1 - 1½ tablespoons mixture on toasted bread slices. Broil 6" from heat until bubbly, 1 - 2 minutes. Serve hot.

19

Corey's Landing Crabmeat Cocktail

Preparation time: 40 minutes
Cooking time: 5 minutes
Refrigeration time: 8 hours or overnight

Makes one 4-cup mold

1	envelope gelatin
2	cans crabmeat, drained and flaked
2	cups mayonnaise
1	cup celery, finely chopped
½	cup onion, finely chopped
½	cup chili sauce
1	tablespoon lemon juice
1	teaspoon salt
½	teaspoon pepper
½	teaspoon Worcestershire sauce
	sliced cucumbers and olives for garnish

Oil one 4-cup jello mold.

Dissolve gelatin in small cup according to package directions. Put dissolved gelatin, lemon juice, salt, pepper, Worcestershire sauce and chili sauce in small sauce pan. Cook, stirring over low heat, 1 - 2 minutes. Remove from heat.

Stir in crabmeat, mayonnaise, celery and onion. Pour mixture into prepared mold. Cover and refrigerate 8 hours or overnight.

Unmold on lettuce-lined platter. Garnish with cucumbers and olives. Serve with assorted crackers.

—————————••●••———————

 In buying and collecting great works of art, John Ringling discovered an exciting challenge and achieved enormous gratification. It not only brought him into the company of the rich and famous, it allowed him to create something of great value and permanence. His ambitious collection ultimately bestowed his beloved Sarasota with a distinctive, cultural character all its own.

—————————••●••———————

Dade County Deviled Eggs

Preparation time: 40 minutes   Makes 24

1	dozen cold hard-boiled eggs, peeled
⅓	cup mayonnaise
1	tablespoon prepared mustard
2	teaspoons minced onion
2 - 3	drops hot sauce
1	tablespoon sweet pickle relish

Cut eggs in half lengthwise. Remove yolks to small mixing bowl. Mash thoroughly. Mix yolks with mayonnaise, mustard and remaining ingredients. Fill egg whites, cover lightly and chill one hour.

St. Croix Liver Pâté

Preparation time: 30 minutes   Makes one 5-cup mold
Chilling time: 8 hours or overnight

1	can beef consommé
1	envelope plain gelatin
¼	cup cold water
2	3-ounce packages cream cheese, softened
1	2" x 4" piece of liverwurst
1	green onion, sliced
½	teaspoon dry mustard
¼	teaspoon Worcestershire sauce
¼	teaspoon pepper

Oil one 5-cup jello mold. Dissolve gelatin according to package directions. Set aside. In small saucepan, heat beef consommé to boiling. Add dissolved gelatin. Put consommé-gelatin mixture in blender. Add cream cheese, liverwurst, onion, dry mustard, Worcestershire sauce and pepper. Blend until mixture is very smooth. Pour into prepared mold. Cover. Chill until firm, 8 hours or overnight.

Unmold and serve with assorted crackers.

Clearwater Crabmeat Stuffed Mushrooms

Preparation time: 40 minutes   Makes 36
Cooking time: 30 minutes

3	**dozen fresh mushrooms**
¼	**teaspoon dry mustard**
½	**cup mayonnaise**
1	**7½-ounce can crabmeat, drained and flaked**
1	**tablespoon chopped parsley**
1	**tablespoon chopped pimiento**
1	**teaspoon capers**

Preheat oven to 350°.

Wash and dry mushrooms. Remove stems. Mix mustard with mayonnaise. Add remaining ingredients and blend well.

Stuff each mushroom cap with 1 - 2 teaspoons stuffing mixture. Bake 20 - 30 minutes.

Asparagus Wrapped with Smoked Salmon

Preparation time: 20 minutes   Makes 10 appetizers

10	**asparagus spears, cooked**
4	**ounces smoked salmon, thinly sliced**
3	**tablespoons Dijon mustard**
3	**tablespoons sugar**
1	**tablespoon vinegar**
3	**tablespoons salad oil**
	salt to taste
	dash of white pepper

Wrap each asparagus spear with smoked salmon slice. Chill. In small bowl, blend remaining ingredients until well mixed. Serve with asparagus as dip.

Antipasto Primavera

Preparation time: 1 hour
Cooking time: 10 minutes
Marinating time: 8 hours or overnight

Serves 8 - 10

Marinade
1	cup olive oil
1½	cups wine vinegar
2	teaspoons salt
¾	teaspoons ground pepper
4	tablespoons sugar
1	clove garlic, minced

Vegetables
3	bell peppers (1 green, 1 red, 1 yellow) cut into ½" strips
1	pound small button mushrooms, cleaned
1	small cauliflower, separated into flowerets
1	bunch green onions, cleaned
1	11-ounce jar pitted black olives, drained

For marinade, put vinegar, oil, sugar, garlic, salt and pepper in a small saucepan. Heat to boil, cook 1 - 2 minutes, stirring. Remove from heat. Cool.

For vegetables, place prepared vegetables in large bowl. Add cooked marinade. Toss with wooden spoon.

Cover and refrigerate several hours or overnight.

To serve, drain before arranging on lettuce-lined serving plate.

Serve with assorted crackers and breads.

Mushrooms Florentine

Preparation time: 30 minutes   Makes 12 - 16
Cooking time: 15 minutes

12 - 16	mushrooms, washed, dried and stems removed
8	tablespoons butter or margarine
1 - 1½	tablespoons onion, minced
1	clove garlic, minced
1	package frozen chopped spinach
¼	teaspoon nutmeg
2	tablespoons Parmesan cheese
	salt and pepper to taste

Preheat oven to 375°.

Melt 6 tablespoons butter. Dip mushroom caps in butter. Place underside up in a greased baking dish. Chop mushroom stems. Sauté with onion, garlic in remaining butter until soft, not brown. Cook and drain spinach. Add to mushroom stems along with remaining ingredients. Fill each mushroom cap. Bake 15 minutes.

Norwegian Flat Bread Canapés

Preparation time: 15 minutes   Serves 6 - 8
Cooking time: 4 minutes

1	stick butter or margarine
½	cup grated fresh Parmesan cheese
2	teaspoons Beau Monde seasoning
2	tablespoons fresh parsley, chopped
½	box of flatbread

Preheat oven to 350°.

Combine first 4 ingredients, mix well. With butter knife spread mixture thinly on each piece of flatbread. Bake on cookie sheet 4 minutes or until light brown. Store in an airtight container.

Quiche Lorraine

Preparation time: 20 minutes
Cooking time: 45 minutes

Makes 1 quiche

1	**9" pie crust**
½	**pound bacon**
1	**onion, thinly sliced**
1	**cup Gruyère cheese, freshly grated**
4	**eggs**
¾	**cup milk**
¾	**cup heavy cream**
⅛	**teaspoon cayenne pepper**
	dash of nutmeg

Preheat oven to 450°.

Bake crust 10 minutes. Remove from oven. Lower heat to 350°.

Fry bacon until crisp, crumble, reserving 2 tablespoons drippings. Sauté onion in drippings until golden brown. Spread onion, bacon and grated cheese in pie shell. Set aside.

Beat eggs, add milk, cream and seasonings. Mix well and add to mixture in pie shell.

Bake on cookie sheet for approximately 35 minutes or until knife inserted in center comes out clean.

Let stand 5 minutes before serving.

* • • • *

John Ringling's varied and consuming interests—in the circus, real estate and the world of art—each received his tireless and devoted attention. As with all his interests, Ringling approached art with tenacity, amassing considerable knowledge which helped him find his way among art professionals. He ultimately achieved national recognition as a collector of museum-quality works and as a respected connoisseur.

* • • • *

Spanikopitas

Preparation time: 1 hour
Cooking time: 15 minutes

Makes 32 triangles

1	17¼-ounce package of frozen puff pastry sheets
1	10-ounce package frozen chopped spinach, thawed and drained
2	large eggs, beaten
1	cup feta cheese
1	medium onion, minced
2	tablespoons parsley, finely chopped
1	egg beaten with 1 teaspoon water
	salt to taste

Preheat oven to 400°.

Thaw pastry for 20 minutes. Roll each sheet into a 12" square and cut each square into 16 3" squares.

Combine spinach, eggs, cheese, onion and parsley. Spoon mixture in center of each square. Brush edges of pastry with egg wash. Fold pastry over to form triangle and seal edges. Brush tops with egg wash and place on ungreased cookie sheet. Bake 15 minutes or until golden brown. Serve hot.

Bacon-Wrapped Water Chestnuts

Preparation time: 15 minutes
Cooking time: 20 minutes

Makes 20

1	6-ounce can water chestnuts
½	pound bacon
1	tablespoon soy sauce
1	tablespoon dry sherry

Preheat oven to 350°.

Wrap ½ slice bacon around each water chestnut, fasten with toothpick. Place water chestnuts in ovenproof dish, brush with mixture of sauce and sherry. Bake 15 - 20 minutes.

Golden Gate Point Blue Cheese Spread

Preparation time: 30 minutes   Makes 2 cups
Cooking Time: 10 minutes

1	tablespoon unflavored gelatin
¼	cup cold water
¼	cup half-and-half cream
¼	cup blue cheese
1	8-ounce package cream cheese, softened
⅛	teaspoon garlic powder
½	teaspoon garlic salt (optional)
½	cup sour cream
2	teaspoons Worcestershire sauce
	olives for garnish

Partially dissolve gelatin in water.

In saucepan over medium heat, combine gelatin with water and stir until gelatin is completely dissolved.

In separate bowl, combine all other ingredients and blend very thoroughly. Stir into gelatin mixture. Pour into lightly greased 2-cup mold.

When set, can be served unmolded or on an attractive serving dish as it is.

Garnish with olives and serve with Melba rounds.

•••••

 As soon as John and Mable Ringling decided to collect works of art and build a museum in 1925, they gathered all available information regarding their shared interest in Italian art and the Old Masters. Having built a considerable knowledge through intense study, skilled advice, and an uncanny memory for detail, John was able to make careful selections. Within six years, the Ringling collection blossomed to over 600 paintings and many times that number of other works of art.

•••••

Zesty Marinated Carrot Sticks

Preparation time: 15 minutes   Makes 1 pound
Cooking time: 15 minutes

2	cups water
½	cup cider vinegar
2	tablespoons sugar
1	teaspoon seasoned salt
⅛ - ¼	teaspoon cayenne pepper
1	pound carrots, cut into 4" sticks

In large sauce pan combine all ingredients except carrots. Bring to a boil. Add carrots and return to a boil for 2 - 3 minutes. Drain. Plunge carrots into a bowl of ice.

Store in a covered container.

Bengal Cream Cheese Spread

Preparation time: 20 minutes   Makes 2 cups

1	8-ounce package cream cheese
3	tablespoons mayonnaise
½	tablespoon curry powder
1	8-ounce jar mango chutney
6	ounces bacon, cooked until crisp and crumbled
6 - 8	scallions, chopped fine

Beat cream cheese until smooth. Add mayonnaise and curry powder.

Spread mixture ½" deep in flat serving dish. Spread chutney over cream cheese mixture.

Sprinkle with crumbled bacon and scallions. Serve with crackers or toast rounds.

Hurricane Horseradish Dip

Preparation time: 10 minutes   Makes 1 cup
Chilling time: 1 hour

1	cup mayonnaise
1	teaspoon horseradish
1	teaspoon tarragon vinegar
1	teaspoon garlic salt
1	teaspoon curry powder
½	teaspoon minced onion

Mix until well blended. Serve with assorted vegetables.

This dip can be refrigerated for up to one week.

Gator Bowl Green Chili Dip

Preparation time: 10 minutes   Makes 2 cups

1	8-ounce package cream cheese, softened
½	pint plus 1 tablespoon sour cream
15	chopped stuffed olives
1	small can diced green chili peppers
½	teaspoon onion salt
¼	teaspoon hot sauce

Combine all ingredients until mixed well.

Serve with tortilla chips.

Mexicana Fruit & Salsa Dip

Preparation time: 45 minutes

Serves 10 - 12

4	plum tomatoes, seeded and diced
1	cup cantaloupe, diced
1	cup watermelon, seeded and diced
1	cup cucumber, peeled, seeded and diced
⅓	cup red onion, chopped fine
1	teaspoon jalapeño pepper, seeded and minced
2	tablespoons fresh lime juice
2	tablespoons coarsely chopped flat leaf parsley or cilantro

Mix ingredients together.

Let stand at room temperature for at least 1 hour.

Serve with tortilla chips.

John Ringling's personal art collection, composed almost entirely of Old Masters, grew at an impressive rate. He purchased up to 20 or more pieces at once, choosing carefully from large collections offered at auction.

Many of Ringling's purchases were works that once adorned the halls of great houses in England and on the Continent. John Ringling derived immense satisfaction from acquiring great works of art which had once hung in the grand salons and ballrooms of important families.

Gulf Coast Guacamole Dip

Preparation time: 15 minutes   Makes 1½ cups

2	medium ripe avocados
3	hard boiled eggs, chopped fine
1	onion grated
1	teaspoon salt
1	teaspoon lemon juice

Mash avocados.

Add chopped eggs, grated onion, salt and lemon juice. Blend well.

Serve with tortilla chips.

Sarasota Bay Shrimp Dip

Preparation time: 20 minutes   Makes 1½ cups

1	6-ounce can small shrimp
2	tablespoons grated onion
2	tablespoons thick french dressing
2	tablespoons mayonnaise
8	ounces cream cheese
	dash of garlic

Blend all ingredients except shrimp. Mix well. Add shrimp.

Chill several hours. Remove from refrigerator at least 1 hour before serving.

Serve with crackers.

Fiesta Nachos

Preparation time: 30 minutes   Serves 12 - 16
Cooking time: 20 minutes

1	**pound ground beef**
1	**medium onion, finely chopped**
½	**teaspoon salt (optional)**
1	**14-ounce can refried beans**
1	**4-ounce can green chilies, drained**
2	**cups Monterey Jack cheese, shredded**
¾	**cup sharp cheddar cheese, shredded**
¾	**cup medium or hot taco sauce**
1	**cup sour cream**
½	**cup green onion, chopped**
1	**cup pitted ripe olives, chopped**
1	**large avocado**
1	**tablespoon lemon or lime juice**

In skillet over medium-high heat brown ground beef and onion. Drain.

In a lightly greased 9" x 13" baking dish, spread refried beans evenly over bottom. Layer with meat, green chilies and cheeses. Drizzle taco sauce over all. Bake 20 minutes or until cheese melts and begins to bubble.

Remove from oven. Cover with dollops of sour cream. Cut avocado in small pieces, toss with lemon or lime juice. Sprinkle green onion, olives and avocado over all. Serve hot with crisp tortilla chips.

This recipe is great for a crowd!

—••●••—

 With exhaustive self-directed study and tireless interest, John Ringling grew to the rank of recognized art collector in a remarkably short time. His collection exhibits a learned appreciation for a range of schools, national cultures and periods.

—••●••—

The facade of The John and Mable Ringling Museum of Art
shows the influence of Italian architecture and classical style.

The gateway arch to John and Mable Ringling's subtropical
estate and Venetian-style mansion, Cà d'Zan, on Sarasota Bay.

A view from the south lawn of Cà d'Zan, John and Mable Ringling's
Sarasota winter mansion.

The bronze statue of **David**, the focal point of the Courtyard
of The John and Mable Ringling Museum of Art.

Soups &
Salads

Old-Fashioned Vegetable Soup

Preparation time: 40 minutes
Cooking time: 45 minutes

Makes 6 - 8 quarts

4	**pounds lean prime beef, cubed**
¼	**cup butter or margarine**
4	**cups onion, chopped**
4	**cups carrots, sliced**
1	**green pepper, chopped**
1	**cup celery tops, chopped**
2	**cups cabbage, chopped**
2	**quarts hot water**
6	**10½-ounce cans beef broth**
1	**tablespoon seasoned salt**
1	**teaspoon pepper, ground**
4	**bay leaves**
½	**teaspoon basil**
4	**cups potatoes, diced**
1	**32-ounce can tomato juice**

Brown beef in butter or margarine. Add onions and heat 5 minutes. Skim fat, if desired.

Add remaining ingredients (except the potatoes and tomato juice) and bring to a boil. Simmer for 30 minutes or until meat is tender.

Add potatoes and tomato juice. Bring to a boil and simmer 10 - 15 additional minutes.

Taste and add additional salt if desired.

This recipe makes several quarts of soup, but it is easy to half the recipe.

Good with hard rolls and pie for dessert.

Bayou Beer Cheese Soup

Preparation time: 30 minutes
Cooking time: 15 minutes

Serves 6 - 8

½	cup butter or margarine
1	cup flour
4	cups hot chicken broth
1½	cups half-and-half cream
16	ounces processed cheese
6	ounces beer
1	tablespoon Worcestershire sauce
¼	cup chives, chopped

In a heavy pan, melt butter. Add flour, blending until smooth. Mixture will be thick. Continue stirring while adding broth and cream. Mix until smooth. Add cheese, beer and Worcestershire sauce. Stir until smooth. Simmer about 15 minutes. Serve hot. Sprinkle with chives.

Buccaneer Broccoli Soup

Preparation time: 30 minutes
Cooking time: 10 minutes

Makes 1½ quarts

1	large bunch broccoli or 2 packages frozen chopped broccoli
3	tablespoons butter
⅓	cup flour
1	cup chicken broth
2	cups milk
¼	teaspoon rosemary
	croutons

In a pan over medium heat, cook broccoli in a small amount of water until tender. Reserve liquid. In another pan over medium heat, melt butter. Add flour, chicken broth and milk, stirring constantly until thickened into a white sauce. Put cooked broccoli and reserved liquid into blender and chop for a few seconds. Then add it to the cream sauce. Heat thoroughly. If soup is too thick, add more milk. Stir in rosemary. Serve with croutons sprinkled on top.

French Onion Soup

Preparation time: 30 minutes

Serves 4 - 6

Baking time: 15 minutes

6	large onions, sliced and separated into rings
½	cup butter
3	cups hot water
5	bouillon cubes
1	can consommé or beef broth, diluted with ½ - 1 cup water
dash	Worcestershire sauce
⅓	cup dry vermouth
1	loaf French bread
10 - 12	ounces Swiss Gruyère cheese

Preheat oven to 350°.

In a skillet sauté onion rings in butter or margarine. When light brown and tender (about 10 minutes) sprinkle with flour. Stir. Add hot water, bouillon cubes and consommé or broth. Stir. Add Worcestershire sauce and dry vermouth to taste.

Toast slices of French bread. Pour soup into individual oven-ware pots, placing bread slices on top of each. Then cover with Swiss Gruyère cheese.

Bake about 15 - 20 minutes, until hot and bubbly.

This makes a good first course or a great lunch.

———— •◦•◦• ————

 For generations of Americans and Europeans, the Ringling name has meant circus, with all its smiles, thrills and hearty laughter. Yet John Ringling also displayed showmanship in other arenas in which he pursued fame and fortune. He was a land developer, an oil man, and corporate entrepreneur as well as an accomplished art connoisseur and collector.

———— •◦•◦• ————

Marco Island Fresh Mushroom Soup

Preparation time: 30 minutes   Serves 6
Cooking time: 10 - 15 minutes

6	tablespoons butter
1½	cups yellow onions, finely minced
½	teaspoon sugar
1	pound fresh mushrooms, ⅓ sliced, ⅔ finely chopped
¼	cup flour
1	cup water
2	cups chicken broth
½	cup dry vermouth
	salt and pepper to taste

In large skillet over medium heat, melt butter. Add onions and sugar and sauté until golden brown. Add mushrooms and sauté 5 minutes. Stir in flour until smooth. Cook 2 minutes, stirring constantly. Add water and stir until smooth. Add remaining ingredients and heat to boiling, stirring constantly. Reduce heat and simmer uncovered 10 - 15 minutes.

Minnesota Wild Rice Soup

Preparation time: 30 minutes   Serves 8 - 10
Cooking time: 15 - 30 minutes

1	medium onion, thinly sliced	2	cups chicken, cooked and cut up
4	ounces fresh mushrooms, chopped	1½	cups wild rice, cooked
3	tablespoons butter or margarine	1	cups half-and-half cream
¼	cup flour	¼	cup dry sherry
4	cups chicken broth		chopped parsley
			salt and pepper to taste

In a soup pan over medium heat, cook onion and mushrooms in butter until onion is transparent. Add flour and cook 10 - 15 minutes. Add chicken broth and cook 10 more minutes. Add remaining ingredients. Simmer on low heat 15 - 30 minutes.

Split Pea Soup

Preparation time: 45 minutes
Cooking time: 6 hours
Soaking time: overnight

Makes 2 - 3 quarts

1	bone with some meat, from 10 - 12 pound ham roast
3	quarts cold water
1	large onion, thinly sliced
2	bay leaves
6 - 8	peppercorns
1	large carrot, grated
1	12-ounce package dried split peas
	salt and pepper to taste
	croutons
	dash of sherry

Place hambone in a soup kettle over low heat. Cover with cold water. Add onion, bay leaves and peppercorns. Simmer 5 hours.

Remove from heat. Take ham off bones. Discard bones and reserve meat.

Place stock in refrigerator overnight. Soak peas in water overnight.

In the morning, skim fat from stock. Return meat to stock. Add carrot and drained peas. Simmer over low heat until peas are pureed and soup is smooth. Season with salt and pepper to taste.

Serve with croutons and a dash of sherry.

----••●•••----

John and Mable Ringling, married in 1905, were in many ways opposites who together formed a balanced union. The one was a brilliant yet cautious, private man; the other, energetic, confident and giving.

----••●•••----

Tarpon Springs Tomato Bisque

Preparation time: 30 minutes
Cooking time: 35 - 40 minutes

Serves 6 - 8

¾	cup onion, chopped
⅔	cup butter or margarine
¾	teaspoon dill seed
1	teaspoon dill weed
1	teaspoon oregano
¼	cup flour

3 - 4	cups canned tomatoes, chopped
3	cups chicken broth
1½	teaspoons salt
¼	teaspoon white pepper
¼	cup parsley, chopped
¼	cup honey
1½	cups half-and-half cream

Sauté onions with butter, dill weed, dill seed and oregano. Add flour and stir for 2 minutes. Add tomatoes and chicken broth and stir slowly. Add salt and pepper. Bring to a boil. Reduce heat and simmer for 15 minutes. Add parsley, honey and half-and-half cream. Simmer for an additional 20 - 30 minutes on lowest heat. Stir and serve.

Barrier Island Shrimp Bisque

Preparation time: 30 minutes

Serves 4

4	tablespoons butter or margarine
¼	cup flour
2	cups milk
1	pound shrimp, peeled, deveined and cut lengthwise
4	green onions, chopped
¼	cup olive oil
11	ounces salsa, medium
¼	cup sherry
1	tablespoon Worcestershire sauce

Melt butter in saucepan over medium heat. Add flour, then milk and stir until smooth and creamy. In a separate skillet sauté shrimp and onions in olive oil until shrimp are opaque. Add shrimp, salsa, sherry and Worcestershire sauce to milk mixture and heat until bubbling. This is good topped with grated cheese and served with garlic toast.

Bay Scallop Chowder

Preparation time: 45 minutes
Cooking time: 40 minutes

Serves 6

2	leeks	1	quart water
1	stalk celery, diced	1	pound bay scallops
2	onions, diced	1	pint cream or half-and-half cream
6	tablespoons butter or margarine	1	tablespoon parsley, chopped
1½	pounds potatoes, peeled and diced		salt and pepper to taste

Wash and cut green leaves off leeks. Cut into fourths, leaving roots on. Wash very well. Dice. Then cut off roots. Set aside.

In a pan over medium heat, sauté diced leeks, celery and onions in butter or margarine until onions are transparent (not brown). Add potatoes, salt and water. Bring to a boil, lower heat and simmer 30 minutes. Before the chowder is served, bring back to a boil and add scallops. In a separate saucepan bring the cream to a boil. Add cream to chowder and stir. Add parsley. Salt and pepper to taste.

Marina Clam Chowder

Preparation time: 40 minutes
Cooking time: 15 minutes

Serves 6 - 8

1	medium onion, chopped	2 - 4	cups canned clams (not drained)
½	cup lean salt pork, cubed	4	cups Idaho potatoes, peeled and cooked
2	tablespoons butter		salt and pepper to taste
2	tablespoons flour		Tabasco Sauce to taste
4	cups milk, scalded		

In a skillet over medium heat, brown onions in salt pork. In a separate pan over medium heat, melt butter, add flour, stirring until smooth. Slowly add milk and stir constantly until thickened. Add clams and clam juice to consistency you prefer. Then add potatoes, salt pork and onion. Heat thoroughly. Before serving, add salt, pepper and Tabasco Sauce to taste.

Florida Keys Oven Fish Chowder

Preparation time: 15 minutes   Serves 10 - 12
Cooking time: 1¼ hours

2	pounds fish (frozen or fresh) like cod, haddock or turbot
4	medium onions, sliced thin
½	cup butter or margarine
5	medium potatoes, peeled and cubed
2	bay leaves
4	cloves
½	teaspoon dry dill weed or seed
2	teaspoons salt
dash	black pepper, freshly ground
1	cup dry white wine
2	cups water, boiling
1 - 2	cups cream (to desired thickness of chowder)

Preheat oven to 375°.

Thaw frozen fish. In a pan over medium heat, sauté onions in butter until limp. Put onions and all ingredients, except cream, into large oven-proof casserole dish. Cover well and bake for 1¼ hours. In a separate saucepan bring cream to scalding point and add to chowder. For a thicker chowder, reduce cream. Break up fish with fork and stir. Serve hot with hard rolls and pie for dessert.

———— ••●••═ ————

 Known to millions of Americans simply as "the circus man," John Nicholas Ringling was, in fact, far more. As a circus promoter, a patron, critic and connoisseur of the arts and an ambitious developer of real estate, he passionately pursued a melding of the popular and the elite.

The tangible results of this cultural convergence were the Ringling Bros. and Barnum & Bailey Circus, as well as an extensive collection of baroque paintings, European decorative art, Italian statuary and his Sarasota mansion, Cà d'Zan.

———— ••●••═ ————

Chilled Cream of Curried Pea Soup

Preparation time: 30 minutes
Cooking time: 20 minutes
Chilling time: 6 - 8 hours or overnight

Serves 4 - 6

1	cup fresh peas, shelled	1	medium onion, sliced
1	small carrot, sliced	1	clove garlic
1	stalk celery with leaves, sliced	1	teaspoon curry powder
1	teaspoon salt	2	cups chicken broth
1	medium potato, sliced	¾	cup heavy cream

Combine vegetables, seasonings and 1 cup chicken broth in a pan. Bring to a boil. Cover. Reduce heat and simmer 15 minutes. Remove from heat and transfer liquid to a blender. Cover and blend on high speed. While blender is running add remainder of chicken broth and ½ cup of the heavy cream. Chill in refrigerator 6 - 8 hours or overnight.

Serve cold. Before serving, whip the remaining ¼ cup heavy cream and use as garnish.

Quick Vichyssoise

Preparation time: 30 minutes
Chilling time: 6 - 8 hours or overnight

Serves 4 - 6

2	small onions, sliced
2	tablespoons butter or margarine
3	chicken bouillon cubes
3	cups water, boiling
2	medium potatoes, peeled and sliced
1	cup heavy cream
4	teaspoons fresh chives or onion greens (garnish)

In a skillet over medium heat sauté onions in butter. In a separate saucepan dissolve chicken bouillon cubes in boiling water. Add potatoes and boil until tender. Put potatoes and onions into blender and blend for 30 seconds. Add heavy cream. Chill in refrigerator 6 - 8 hours or overnight. Serve cold with chives or onion greens as garnish.

Venice Vichyssoise

Preparation time: 50 minutes
Chilling time: 6 - 8 hours or overnight

Serves 8 - 10

3	large leeks (white tips only)	1½	tablespoons salt
3	tablespoons butter	1	quart half-and-half cream
3	small onions, sliced	½	cup heavy cream
8	medium potatoes, peeled and sliced		chives, finely chopped for garnish
6	cups chicken broth		

Wash and thinly slice leeks. Melt butter in large kettle. Add onions and leeks and cook until limp. Add potatoes and cover with chicken broth. Cook gently until potatoes are tender. Remove from heat. Put in blender or food processor and blend until smooth. Return to heat and add half-and-half. Remove from heat and cool. When soup is cool, add heavy cream to right consistency. If still too thick, add half-and-half. Chill 6 - 8 hours or overnight. Serve topped with chives as garnish.

Carrot Vichyssoise

Preparation time: 45 minutes
Chilling time: 6 - 8 hours or overnight

Serves 4

2	tablespoons butter	⅛	teaspoon pepper
2	bunches scallions, sliced	½	cup light cream
2	cups seasoned chicken broth	1	teaspoon chopped chives or parsley
2	cups carrots, cooked and sliced		diced cucumber or chopped onion
½	teaspoon salt		sour cream

Melt butter in a small saucepan. Add scallions and cook over medium heat for 5 minutes. Add 1 cup of the chicken broth and bring to a boil. Cover and simmer over low heat for 15 minutes. Pour scallions and broth mixture into blender. Add remaining cup of broth, carrots and seasonings. Cover and puree until contents are smooth, about 1 minute. Add light cream and chill thoroughly. To serve, top with chives or parsley and a dollop of sour cream. This soup may also be heated in a heavy saucepan, and served hot.

Andalusian Gazpacho

Preparation time: 45 minutes

Chilling time: 4 - 6 hours

Serves 8

3	tomatoes, peeled and sliced
1	cucumber, peeled, seeded and sliced
1	medium onion, quartered
1	clove garlic, minced
1	green pepper, seeded and sliced
¼	cup dry bread crumbs
½	teaspoon salt
2	tablespoon olive oil
2	tablespoon vinegar
2	cups tomato juice
dash	cayenne pepper

Whirl tomatoes, cucumber, onion, garlic and green pepper in a blender. Add bread crumbs and chill 1 hour.

When chilled, blend in salt, olive oil, vinegar, tomato juice and cayenne pepper. Chill until serving time.

To serve, pour soup into bowls and add 1 ice cube per bowl. Garnish with diced cucumber or chopped onion and a dollop of sour cream.

 As part of the Ringling Bros. Circus, John Ringling achieved international renown. In addition, he achieved recognition outside the big top. He was widely respected and enjoyed the company of bankers, railroad barons and other men of fortune. He schooled himself in the arts, and became established in the art buyers' market in New York and London. During his 25 years in Sarasota, he owned real estate properties as distant as Montana and Oklahoma. While at home, he became the city's key developer of the 1920s. In all, John Ringling held positions in 35 different companies during his lifetime.

Patio Pear Salad

Preparation time: 25 minutes

Chilling time: 8 hours or overnight

Makes 10" mold

1	29-ounce can sliced pears
1	6-ounce package lime gelatin
2	8-ounce packages cream cheese, softened
2	tablespoons half-and-half cream
	parsley for garnish

Drain pears, reserving juice. Measure reserved juice; if necessary, add water to make 2 cups. Heat this liquid to a boil in a saucepan. Dissolve gelatin in hot juice. Chill.

Cream cheese with half-and-half cream. Add gelatin which has been chilled but not set. Mash pears and fold into gelatin along with whipped cream. Pour into 2-quart mold and chill until firm. When ready to serve, unmold onto platter and garnish with parsley.

St. Lucie Romaine Strawberry Salad

Preparation time: 15 minutes

Serves 8

Dressing

¾	cup mayonnaise
¼	cup milk
2	tablespoons white wine vinegar
⅓	cup sugar
1½	tablespoons poppy seed

Salad

1	bunch romaine lettuce, washed, drained, torn into bitesize pieces
1	pint sliced fresh strawberries (more if desired)
1	medium red onion, thinly sliced, separated into rings

For dressing, mix all ingredients until well blended. For salad, put ingredients in salad bowl, drizzle with dressing, toss, serve.

Orange Bowl Mandarin Salad

Preparation time: 15 - 20 minutes

Serves 4 - 6

Dressing
- ¼ cup olive oil
- 2 tablespoons vinegar
- 2 tablespoons sugar
- ½ teaspoon salt
- ½ teaspoon Tabasco Sauce
- pepper to taste

Salad
- 1 large bowl of mixed fresh salad greens
- 3 green onions, thinly sliced
- 1 11-ounce can mandarin oranges, drained

Almonds (optional)
- 2 tablespoons sugar (optional)
- ¼ cup slivered almonds (optional)

Mix dressing ingredients. Toss with greens, onion and oranges. Serve on individual chilled salad plates.

For an optional delicate and sweet almond flavor, prepare sweetened almonds. Put sugar in small nonstick skillet and cook stirring over low heat.

When sugar begins to melt, add slivered almonds. Continue stirring to coat almonds with melted sugar, 1 - 2 minutes.

Remove from heat, spoon almonds onto wax paper, cool. Sprinkle over salad.

Mandarin Chicken Salad with Melon

Preparation time: 30 minutes   Serves 6

Salad
2	whole large chicken breasts (about 2 pounds), cooked (roasted, baked or grilled) and cubed
2	cups celery, sliced
5	ounces slivered almonds
2	11-ounce cans mandarin oranges, drained
3	medium cantaloupes, halved, seeded and chilled

Dressing
¾	cup sour cream
¾	cup mayonnaise
2	tablespoons lemon juice
2	tablespoons fresh ginger, grated
1	tablespoon fresh orange peel, grated
½	teaspoon salt
	dash of nutmeg (no more than ⅛ teaspoon)

In large bowl, combine chicken, celery, almonds and oranges.

To make the dressing, in small bowl blend together sour cream, mayonnaise, lemon juice, ginger, orange peel, salt and nutmeg. Add just enough dressing to chicken mixture to coat well.

Chill and serve in cantaloupe halves.

———————•••••———————

 The wife of circus magnate John Ringling, Mable Burton Ringling was not one to sit idle during the leisure winter months of Sarasota life. Polishing her skills with tutoring in English, diction and the arts, Mable soon emerged as an accomplished, admired woman of Sarasota society. She frequently entertained the women of Sarasota, 60 or more at a time, with lunch and an afternoon of bridge.

———————•••••———————

Symphony Spinach Strawberry Salad

Preparation time: 20 minutes

Serves 6 - 8

Dressing

½	cup sugar
¼	teaspoon paprika
2	tablespoons sesame seeds
1	tablespoon poppy seeds
1½	teaspoons onion, finely chopped
¼	teaspoon Worcestershire sauce
½	cup vegetable oil
¼	cup cider vinegar
6	strips bacon, crisply fried and crumbled

Salad

6	cups fresh spinach, washed, drained and torn into bitesize pieces
1	pint fresh strawberries, hulled and sliced

For dressing, blend sugar, sesame seeds, onion, paprika and Worcestershire sauce in blender or food processor. Add vinegar. With machine running, slowly drizzle oil into mixture, blend until smooth and creamy. Stir in bacon. For salad, toss ingredients in salad bowl, drizzle with dressing. Serve.

Belgian Endive Salad with Gorgonzola Dressing

Preparation time: 15 minutes

Serves 4

1	pound Belgian endive
4	tablespoons Gorgonzola cheese, room temperature
6	tablespoons plain yogurt
2	tablespoons brandy
	pinch of cayenne pepper

Trim, wash and dry endive leaves. Slice in half lengthwise, arrange on salad plates. In small bowl, using a fork, mash cheese and yogurt well. Add brandy and cayenne pepper. To serve, spoon dressing over endive leaves.

Tableside Caesar Salad

Preparation time: 30 minutes   Serves 10 - 12

3	heads romaine lettuce
1	head iceberg or escarole lettuce
¼	cup olive oil
2	large cloves garlic
3	anchovy fillets
½	teaspoon English hot mustard powder
⅛	cup lemon juice
½	cup red wine vinegar
	dash Tabasco Sauce
1	cup croutons
½	cup grated Parmesan cheese

Several hours prior to preparation, wash lettuce and break into bitesize pieces. Place in refrigerator to crisp.

Place 1 tablespoon of oil in large salad bowl. Using 2 forks (crossing the tines), mash garlic and anchovies in oil. Add remaining oil, mustard, lemon juice, vinegar and Tabasco Sauce. Blend well.

Pat lettuce dry on paper towel.

Put lettuce, croutons and cheese in salad bowl. Drizzle with dressing, toss well to coat. Serve immediately.

Hints for Caesar Salad:

You can never toss a Caesar salad too much.

Do not use the large fork and spoon designed for tossing salads when tossing a Caesar. It is better to use 2 dinner forks, in a circular motion, pulling the lettuce from bottom of the bowl toward you. Allow lettuce to fall lightly when lifting forks.

There should never be any dressing left in the bottom of a Caesar salad bowl.

Asparagus Grapefruit Salad

Preparation time: 30 minutes

Serves 4 - 6

Chilling time: 1 - 2 hours

Salad
1	pound asparagus, washed and trimmed of tough ends
1	pink grapefruit

Vinaigrette Dressing
2	tablespoons raspberry vinegar
1	tablespoon honey
⅛	teaspoon salt
¼	cup safflower oil
1	teaspoon minced packaged chives, or 1 tablespoon fresh chives

Cook asparagus in an 8" or 10" skillet with ⅓ cup water until crisp tender, about 5 - 7 minutes. Blanch under cold water and wrap in paper towels. Chill. Section grapefruit over bowl reserving at least 2 tablespoons of juice.

To make vinaigrette, whisk together reserved grapefruit juice, raspberry vinegar, honey and salt. Slowly whisk in oil until thickened. Set aside.

Arrange chilled asparagus spears on salad plates. Garnish with grapefruit sections. Drizzle with vinaigrette and sprinkle with chives.

Each of John and Mable Ringling's homes was elegantly appointed and well staffed. In Sarasota, seven live-in servants included two housemaids, two housemen, a cook, a butler, and Mable's personal maid. One chauffeur and a crew of groundskeepers completed the household. In their moves between homes in Sarasota, New York and Alpine, New Jersey, the Ringlings didn't take their servants and silver with them, as was the custom of the day. Their residences, therefore, always remained perfectly polished and prepared, awaiting their return.

Coral Gables Garden Potato Salad

Preparation time: 45 minutes   Serves 8
Refrigeration time: 6 hours or overnight

Dressing		Potato Salad	
1½	cups sour cream	4	cups peeled, diced red potatoes
½	cup mayonnaise	1	cup diced cucumber
¼	cup vinegar	3	tablespoons chopped green onions
¾	teaspoon celery seed	1½	teaspoons salt
¾	teaspoon dill weed	½	teaspoons pepper
1	teaspoon prepared mustard	3	diced hard boiled eggs

In bowl, combine dressing ingredients.

Boil potatoes. In separate bowl, add dressing to warm diced potatoes and mix gently. Add all other ingredients. Mix thoroughly.

Refrigerate at least 6 hours before serving to blend flavors.

Chive Potato Salad

Preparation time: 30 minutes   Serves 8 - 10
Refrigeration time: 4 hours

2	pounds unpeeled red potatoes, cooked and chopped
¾	cup mayonnaise
¼	cup chopped chives
3	teaspoons Dijon mustard
½	teaspoon salt
¼	teaspoon pepper

Combine mayonnaise, chives, mustard, salt and pepper. Mix well. In a large bowl, add the dressing mixture to the chopped potatoes and mix gently. Let stand at room temperature for one hour covered. Refrigerate 4 hours before serving.

Shrimp & Rice Salad

Preparation time: 40 minutes

Marinating time: 2 hours

Serves 6 - 8

2	pounds shrimp, shelled, deveined
1	green pepper, seeded, diced
8	black olives, thickly sliced
1½	cups rice, cooked
	lettuce leaves
1	large tomato, diced
1	small cucumber, diced

Dressing

1	cup olive oil
1¼	cup tarragon vinegar
1½	teaspoon salt
½	teaspoon pepper
½	teaspoon garlic, minced
2	tablespoons onion, grated
2	teaspoons capers, chopped

Combine shrimp, green pepper and olives in a large bowl. To make the dressing, beat together the olive oil, vinegar, salt, pepper, garlic, onion and capers in a small bowl. Pour dressing over shrimp mixture and marinate for 2 hours. Before serving, add rice and toss lightly. Serve on lettuce-lined dish, surrounded by diced tomatoes and cucumbers.

———————————•◦•◦•———————————

 During the 1920s, John and Mable Ringling enjoyed celebrity status among their neighbors in Sarasota. Their activities were widely reported following their fall arrival each year in their private Pullman car. John stepped into key leadership roles in local financial affairs, and soon became Sarasota's prominent millionaire-entrepreneur and a recognized art patron. All Sarasota came to the Ringling mansion—to luncheons, yachting parties and musicales—to be charmed by their smiling, unpretentious hostess, Mable.

———————————•◦•◦•———————————

Asheville Salad

Preparation time: 30 minutes
Refrigeration time: 2 - 3 hours or overnight

Serves 8

2	**tablespoons plain gelatin**
½	**cup cold water**
1	**13-ounce can cream of tomato soup**
2	**3-ounce packages cream cheese softened at room temperature**
1	**cup mayonnaise**
½	**cup celery, diced**
¼	**cup onion, diced**
¼	**cup green pepper, diced**
½	**cup stuffed olives, sliced**
16	**medium shrimp, cooked and peeled (optional)**

Soften gelatin in cold water and reserve.

Bring soup to a boil in medium saucepan over medium-high heat. Add softened cream cheese and stir until smooth. Add gelatin softened in cold water. Stir and remove from heat. When mixture is lukewarm, add mayonnaise, chopped vegetables and shrimp.

Pour into 8 individual molds or 8" ring mold. Cover, refrigerate until firm, at least 3 - 4 hours.

Unmold and serve on lettuce-lined serving platter.

Asheville salad is best served from individual molds for luncheon, or from a ring mold for dinner as an accompaniment to rare roast beef or leg of lamb.

Mangrove Island Marinated Cucumbers

Preparation time: 30 minutes

Marinating time: 2 - 3 hours

Makes 2 quarts

7	**cups garden cucumbers, thinly sliced**
1	**medium onion, thinly sliced**
1	**small green pepper, sliced**
2	**tablespoons salt**
1	**cup cider or tarragon vinegar**
2	**cups sugar**
1	**tablespoon celery seed**

Combine first 4 ingredients and let stand 2 hours in a cool place or refrigerator.

After standing, drain well. Combine vinegar, sugar and celery seed. Stir until sugar dissolves. Pour over cucumbers and serve.

This salad, refrigerated, keeps well up to one week.

Florida Tomatoes with Red Wine Vinaigrette

Preparation time: 20 minutes

Serves 4 - 6

3	**large, ripe tomatoes**
2	**tablespoons onion, minced**
¼	**cup basil, minced**
2	**tablespoons olive oil**
2	**tablespoons water**
2	**cloves garlic, minced**
2	**tablespoons red wine vinegar**
¼	**teaspoon Dijon mustard**
	black pepper to taste

Slice tomatoes. Mix remaining ingredients and pour over tomatoes.

Gulf Stream Spinach Salad

Preparation time: 30 minutes
Cooking time: 10 minutes

Serves 6

Salad
½	**pound bacon**
1	**package fresh spinach**
4	**large hard boiled eggs, finely chopped**
1	**small red onion, separated into rings**

Dressing
½	**cup sugar**
½	**cup vinegar**
2	**tablespoons reserved bacon drippings**
½	**teaspoon salt**
1	**large raw egg (optional)**

Fry bacon crisply, reserving 2 tablespoons drippings. Crumble.

Wash and stem spinach. Pat dry on paper towels. Toss together spinach, bacon, eggs and onion slices.

Mix dressing ingredients together and toss with salad.

––––––––••••••––––––––

 The Ringling brothers' travel habits were governed by the circus calendar. At the season's close each year, the families of John and Charles Ringling would turn south toward Sarasota, where they each kept winter homes. Rather than brave the adventure of overland auto travel, the two families journeyed in grand style by rail. Catered to by their butler and personal cook, John and Mable Ringling traveled comfortably in their own private Pullman rail car.

––––––––••••••––––––––

Sweet Fruit Dressing

Preparation time: 15 minutes   Makes about 1½ cups

½	cup sugar
1	teaspoon salt
1	teaspoon dry mustard
1	teaspoon celery seed
1	teaspoon paprika
1	teaspoon onion, grated or finely chopped
1	cup salad oil
¼	cup vinegar

Mix dry ingredients together. Add onion. Alternately add oil and vinegar, adding vinegar last.

Pour over your favorite fresh sliced fruit.

Citrus Juice Dressing

Preparation time: 15 minutes   Makes 1 cup

1	large egg
1	cup sugar
	juice of 1 orange
	juice of 1 lemon
	juice of 1 lime
1	teaspoon grated lemon or lime zest

In a small saucepan, combine sugar and egg. Blend well. Add juices and zest. Bring to a boil over low heat, stirring constantly.

Serve over your favorite sliced fresh fruit in a large bowl or on salad plates.

Store covered in refrigerator.

Thousand Island Dressing

Preparation time: 10 minutes   Makes 1¾ cups

1	cup mayonnaise
½	cup chili sauce
2	tablespoons stuffed olives, minced
1	tablespoon green pepper, chopped
1	tablespoon onion, minced or finely chopped
¼	cup heavy cream

Mix all ingredients together and chill before serving.

Roquefort Dressing

Preparation time: 10 minutes   Makes about 2½ cups
Refrigeration time: 2 - 3 hours

½	cup Roquefort cheese or domestic blue cheese, crumbled
1	cup mayonnaise
1	cup cultured sour cream
4	teaspoons vinegar
2	teaspoons salt
¼	teaspoon freshly ground pepper
1½	tablespoons chopped dried parsley (or 4½ tablespoons fresh)
1	teaspoon dried tarragon (or 1 tablespoon fresh)
1	teaspoon sugar (optional)

Combine mayonnaise and sour cream. Add all other ingredients except cheese, mix well. Gradually add cheese and mix with other ingredients. Chill for several hours before serving.

Festive French Dressing

Preparation time: 15 minutes   Makes about 2 cups

1	**cup olive oil**
⅓	**cup sugar**
⅓	**cup chili sauce**
⅓	**cup vinegar**
2	**teaspoons salt**
1	**teaspoon paprika**
	juice of 1 lemon
⅓	**medium onion, grated or finely chopped**

Blend ingredients in a small mixing bowl or on low setting of a blender.

Store covered in the refrigerator.

Creamy Lemon Dressing

Preparation time: 5 minutes   Makes 2 cups

1	**pint sour cream**
2	**teaspoons dry dill weed (or 2 tablespoons fresh)**
3	**tablespoons fresh lemon juice**

Combine ingredients in small bowl and mix well. Store covered in the refrigerator.

Throughout 25 loving years of marriage to John Ringling until her death in 1929, Mable Ringling accepted the firmly ingrained habits and reserved nature of her older husband. In Mable, John found the affection, companionship and support he so desired.

Meat

Thunderdome Beef Bourguignonne

Preparation time: 1 hour
Cooking time: 2½ - 3 hours

Serves 8

Bouquet Garni

6	whole cloves
2	garlic cloves, minced
½	teaspoon thyme
2	bay leaves
1	slice of orange peel
⅛	teaspoon nutmeg

Beef

¼	pound lean salt pork
4	tablespoons butter or margarine
2	small onions, chopped
1	pound fresh mushrooms, sliced
3	pounds filet mignon or sirloin, cubed
1	tablespoon flour
½	teaspoon salt
2	cups very warm Burgundy wine
1 - 2	tablespoons tomato paste

Make a bouquet garni by blending cloves, garlic, thyme, bay leaves, orange peel and nutmeg. Place in cheesecloth and tie.

Brown salt pork in butter in a Dutch oven. Remove with slotted spoon and set aside. Brown onions in same oven. Remove and set aside. Sauté mushrooms in same Dutch oven. Remove and set aside.

To Dutch oven add beef sprinkled with flour and salt. Brown. Add salt pork, wine and bouquet garni. Cover and cook slowly for 2½ - 3 hours, or until meat is tender.

Just before serving, add tomato paste, reserved onions and mushrooms. Serve hot.

Excellent when accompanied by unbuttered French bread for dunking, a green salad or a lettuce, grapefruit and avocado salad and red wine. It's a rich meal, so sherbet is a good choice for dessert.

Barbecued Flank Steak

Preparation time: 15 minutes
Marinating time: 1 hour or overnight
Cooking time: 10 minutes

Serves 4 - 6

1	flank steak, about 2 pounds
1	cup barbecue sauce
3	tablespoons steak sauce

Dry steak with paper towel and place in a shallow pan. Combine sauces in small bowl and spread over steak. Refrigerate overnight, or a minimum of one hour.

Preheat oven to broil.

Using a sharp knife, lightly score steak in crisscross lines, forming a diamond pattern. Baste with marinade. Broil 3" from heat for 5 minutes. Turn steak, baste again and broil for an additional 5 minutes. To serve, cut steak in thin, diagonal slices. If desired, use pan drippings for sauce.

Roast Beef Tenderloin aux Champignons

Preparation time: 15 minutes
Cooking time: 1¼ hour

Serves 8 - 10

3 - 4	pound tenderloin roast, larded
1	cup beef broth
2	tablespoons butter or margarine
½	pound fresh mushrooms, sliced
	salt and pepper to taste

Preheat oven to 400°.

Place meat, larded side up, in shallow pan. Salt and pepper the top. Bake 1¼ hour for medium doneness. Adjust time for rare or medium well. While roast is cooking, sauté mushrooms in butter or margarine in small saucepan. To serve, add broth and sautéed mushrooms to pan juices. Pour over meat.

Traditional Beef Stew

Preparation time: 30 minutes   Serves 8 - 10
Cooking time: 5 hours

1½	pounds top quality stewing beef, cubed
1	small bunch of carrots, peeled and cut into 1" pieces
1	cup celery, cut into 1" pieces
3	medium onions, quartered
1	tablespoon each salt, sugar and tapioca
1	large can tomatoes, chopped but not drained
3 - 4	medium russet potatoes, peeled and cubed
	fresh ground pepper, to taste

Preheat oven to 250°.

Place all ingredients in a heavy Dutch oven. Cover and bake for 5 hours, or until meat is tender.

Beef Stroganoff

Preparation Time: 30 minutes   Serves 6 - 8
Cooking time: 2 hours

1½	pounds round steak, ¾" thick, cut into strips or cubes
2	tablespoons butter or margarine
¾	cup water
1	large can whole or sliced mushrooms
1	envelope dried onion soup mix
2	tablespoons flour
1	cup sour cream

In a large skillet, brown meat a few pieces at a time in butter or margarine. Add water, mushrooms and soup mix. Cover, bring to a boil, then cook over low heat for about 2 hours, or until meat is tender. Can be prepared in advance to this point and cooled in the refrigerator, if desired. When ready to serve, reheat, then add blended flour and sour cream. Do not boil. Serve over noodles, white rice or wild rice, with a green salad and French bread.

Savory Beef Brisket

Preparation time: 20 minutes
Marinating time: overnight
Cooking time: 5 hours

Serves 8 - 10

5	pounds brisket, trimmed
	Worcestershire sauce
2	tablespoons liquid smoke
2	tablespoons vinegar
1	teaspoon garlic
1	teaspoon salt
1	teaspoon onion salt
1	teaspoon seasoned salt
1	teaspoon pepper
1	teaspoon meat tenderizer
⅓	cup brown sugar

The night before cooking, place a large sheet of heavy-duty foil over a shallow, oven-proof pan. After rubbing brisket on both sides with Worcestershire sauce, place meat on foil. Combine remaining ingredients, pour over brisket and seal with the foil. Refrigerate overnight.

The next day, preheat oven to 200° and bake 5 hours or more. Open foil during the last hour to check for tenderness and to brown. Remove from oven and allow to cool 15 minutes in the pan. Transfer to meat platter and slice across the grain. Remove fat from pan juices and pour remaining juices over meat.

Can be frozen. Defrost. Bring to room temperature and reheat in microwave or regular oven.

———— •●•●• ————

 The John and Mable Ringling Museum of Art, completed in 1929, was designed by John H. Phillips to resemble the villa of a noble Italian family. It stands in an expansive park setting on Sarasota Bay, the formality of its design drawing on architectural designs from the 15th to 18th centuries.

———— •●•●• ————

Midnight Pass Meat Loaf

Preparation time: 40 minutes
Cooking time: 45 minutes

Serves 4

Meat Loaf
1	pound lean ground beef
1	large egg, lightly beaten
4	tablespoons fine bread crumbs
1	tablespoon fresh parsley, minced
¼	cup water
2	tablespoons onion, chopped
2	tablespoons horseradish
1	teaspoon salt
⅛	teaspoon pepper

Sauce
3	tablespoons catsup
½	cup chili sauce
1	teaspoon Worcestershire sauce
½	teaspoon dry mustard
	dash Tabasco Sauce

Preheat oven to 350°.

Combine meat mixture ingredients and shape into 4 oblong loaves. Place in greased shallow baking pan, not touching.

Combine sauce ingredients and spread over tops and sides of loaves. Bake uncovered for 45 minutes, basting 2 or 3 times with drippings.

Can be frozen after cooking. Defrost. Bring to room temperature and reheat in microwave or regular oven.

Portrait of the Archduke Ferdinand
Peter Paul Rubens, 1635, oil on canvas.

The Rubens Gallery at The John and Mable Ringling Museum of Art
exhibits 4 cartoons from *The Triumph of the Eucharist* series, painted
by Peter Paul Rubens and his Studio about 1625.

Abraham and Melchizedek
Peter Paul Rubens and Studio, c. 1625, oil on canvas (detail).

The Astor Gallery was purchased by John Ringling at the auction of the
Vincent Astor mansion. Built in 1894 in the style of a 16th-century French salon, it now
displays antique fans and other heirloom collections at the Ringling Museum.

Swedish Meat Balls

Preparation time: 30 minutes
Cooking time: 1½ hours

Makes 96 small meatballs

1	pound each ground veal, beef and pork
1	cup fresh bread, finely torn, soaked in 1 cup cream
2	large eggs, beaten
2	tablespoons onion, grated
1	teaspoon salt
⅛	teaspoon each pepper and nutmeg
½	cup hot water

Preheat oven to 250°.

Gently mix all ingredients. Form into small balls and brown in oil. Place in shallow baking dish. Add hot water. Cover and bake for about 1½ hours, or until meat balls are tender.

Hungarian Goulash

Preparation time: 45 minutes
Cooking time: 2 - 3 hours

Serves 8

2	pounds stewing beef	1	teaspoon paprika
1	cup onions, diced	2	teaspoon salt
	garlic powder to taste	1	tablespoon brown sugar
¾	cups catsup	1	teaspoon dry mustard
¼	cup Worcestershire sauce	3¼	cups water
1	teaspoon vinegar	2	tablespoons flour

Brown meat. Add onions and garlic powder and sauté until onions are lightly browned. Combine catsup, Worcestershire sauce, vinegar, paprika, salt, sugar and mustard. Stir into meat. Add 3 cups of water and simmer, covered, 2 - 3 hours, or until meat is tender. Whisk 2 tablespoons of flour with ¼ cup cold water and use to thicken goulash.

Serve over noodles or rice. Can be frozen.

Westchester Ham Loaf

Preparation time: 40 minutes
Cooking time: 1½ - 2 hours

Serves 8

Ham Loaf

3	pounds ground meat (either 1 pound ham and 2 pounds pork, or 1 pound ham, 1 pound pork and 1 pound beef)
¾	cup milk
¼	cup catsup
1	teaspoon prepared mustard
2	large eggs
½	cup crackers, crushed
½	cup cornflakes, crushed
1½	teaspoons Worcestershire sauce
	fresh ground pepper to taste

Sauce

½	cup vegetable oil
¼	cup vinegar
¼	cup sugar
¼	cup tomato soup
¼	cup prepared mustard
1	large egg yolk

Preheat oven to 325°.

Place ground meats in a large bowl. By hand, work in remaining ham loaf ingredients. Form into a loaf in a 9" x 13" pan. Bake 1½ - 2 hours.

In a small saucepan, combine sauce ingredients and cook over medium heat for 10 minutes.

Let stand for a few minutes before slicing. Serve with sauce and Pickled Peach Garnish (see Index).

Ham & Broccoli Rolls with Rice

Preparation time: 40 minutes
Cooking time: 30 minutes

Serves 4 - 8

Rolls

8	slices cooked ham, ⅛" thick
1	10-ounce package broccoli spears, cooked and drained
1	tablespoon butter or margarine, melted
2	cups rice
	fresh parsley

Sauce

2	tablespoons butter or margarine
2	tablespoons flour
¼	teaspoon salt
1	cup milk
½	cup sour cream
1	teaspoon chives
2	tablespoons prepared mustard
1	tablespoon fresh parsley, chopped

Preheat oven to 400°.

Roll 1 slice of ham around 1 or 2 broccoli spears. Arrange in shallow pan. Brush with melted butter. Cover and bake for 20 minutes.

Cook rice according to package directions.

For sauce, melt 2 tablespoons butter and blend in flour, salt and milk. Cook and stir until thickened. Add sour cream, chives and mustard.

Spoon rice on platter. Cover with ham rolls. Ladle on sauce and garnish with parsley.

Great Lakes Pork & Wild Rice Casserole

Preparation time: 30 minutes   Serves 4
Soaking time: 1 hour
Cooking time: 1½ - 2 hours

4	**heaping tablespoons wild rice**
4	**pork chops, about 1" thick**
2	**tablespoons butter or margarine**
4	**slices onion, ½" thick**
4	**slices tomato, ½" thick**
	salt and pepper to taste
½	**cup water**

Rinse wild rice several times. Place in a small bowl, cover with warm water and soak 1 hour.

Preheat oven to 325°.

In a skillet, brown chops in butter, then place in baking dish. On each chop place a slice of onion, a slice of tomato and a dash of salt and pepper. Drain rice and arrange around chops. Add water to drippings in skillet and pour around edges of baking dish.

Cover tightly and bake 1½ - 2 hours or until chops are very tender and rice is cooked, adding more water if necessary.

If available, use wild rice grown in a wild rice lake. It's fluffier than the cultivated rice available in supermarkets today.

The 21 galleries of The John and Mable Ringling Museum of Art are arranged in a U-shape around the central courtyard. Each gallery is adorned with architectural details the Ringlings purchased in Italy, such as columns and door frames. Great bronze doors in the Museum's entrance foyer once adorned the Astor home in New York.

Backyard Pork Kebabs

Preparation time: 35 minutes   Serves 8
Cooking time: 45 minutes

	Kebabs			Sauce
4	pork tenderloins, cut into 1" pieces	1½	cups orange juice
		2	teaspoons lemon juice
1	fresh pineapple, peeled and cut into ½" cubes	1	teaspoon each salt and ginger
		¼	cup dark molasses
		4	tablespoons corn starch
		2	teaspoons rum

Preheat oven to 325°.

Alternate pork and pineapple on 12 skewers.

In a saucepan, combine sauce ingredients except rum, and cook, stirring, over low heat until thickened. Remove from heat. Stir in rum. Brush sauce on kebabs and bake in a large baking pan about 45 minutes or until pork is tender, turning once and basting several times.

Countrytime Spareribs

Preparation time: 30 minutes   Serves 4
Cooking time: 1½ hours

16	country pork ribs	2	tablespoons soy sauce
½	cup brown sugar	½	teaspoon garlic powder
⅓	cup each catsup and white vinegar	2	teaspoons ground ginger
			salt and pepper to taste

Preheat oven to 450°.

Line a 9" x 13" pan with heavy duty foil. Place ribs in pan and bake 15 minutes. Remove from oven and pour off fat. Lower oven temperature to 325°. Blend remaining ingredients. Pour over ribs. Return ribs to oven and bake 1¼ hours or until tender.

Masterpiece Marinated Pork Roast

Preparation time: 20 minutes
Marinating time: 5 hours or overnight
Cooking time: 3 hours

Serves 10 - 12

½	cup each soy sauce and dry sherry	1½	teaspoons thyme
2	cloves garlic, minced	1	tablespoon dry mustard
1	teaspoon ginger	4 - 5	pound pork loin, boned and rolled

Preheat oven to 325°.

In a small bowl, combine all ingredients except roast. Place pork loin and marinade in a large plastic bag, close tightly. Let meat marinate in refrigerator for 5 hours or overnight, turning occasionally to distribute marinade. When ready to cook, remove loin from bag, saving liquid for basting. Place pork loin in pan and bake, uncovered for about 3 hours, or until meat thermometer reaches 175°. Baste frequently.

Serve with Curried Fruit Garnish (see Index).

Orlando Roast Leg of Lamb

Preparation time: 30 minutes
Marinating time: overnight
Cooking time: 2 hours

Serves 8 - 10

4	pound leg of lamb, boned, rolled, tied	1	teaspoon each paprika, salt and pepper
1	lemon, cut in half	½	teaspoon garlic powder
1	10-ounce jar mint jelly	1	can beef consommé (for gravy)
1	tablespoon powdered ginger		

The day before roasting, remove excess fat from lamb. Cut roast in several places with tip of sharp knife. Rinse well and rub with lemon. Mix jelly with seasonings and completely cover meat with this marinade. Refrigerate overnight. Preheat oven to 300°. Roast 30 - 35 minutes per pound, basting occasionally. Roast and sauce will be dark brown. Pour off fat and mix consommé with drippings. Serve au jus.

Spiced Lamb Shanks in White Wine Sauce

Preparation time: 30 minutes
Cooking time: 2½ hours

Serves 4 - 6

4 - 6	**lamb shanks (½ - ¾ pound each) trimmed of fat**
	olive oil (to coat shanks)
2	**medium onions, cut into ¼" slices**
1	**teaspoon ground allspice**
½	**teaspoon nutmeg**
1	**teaspoon salt**
½	**teaspoon pepper**
¼	**cup dry white wine**
3	**cups canned whole tomatoes, chopped**

Preheat oven to 400°.

Lightly coat lamb shanks with olive oil. Arrange in 9" x 13" baking dish. Bake in 400° oven for 30 minutes, turning once.

Reduce oven setting to 350°. Remove lamb from oven. Cover with onion slices, allspice, nutmeg, salt and pepper. Pour wine and tomatoes over all.

Return lamb to oven and bake for 2 hours or until tender, basting frequently.

Serve with hot buttered egg noodles. Can be frozen. Defrost, bring to room temperature and reheat in slow oven or microwave.

*David, an 18-foot monumental bronze sculpture dominates the west end of the courtyard of the Ringling Museum. It was cast in Naples to commemorate the birth of Michelangelo. John Ringling bought the statue in 1925 and shipped it to Sarasota, along with tons of other statues, columns, marble doorways and other fragments of buildings. **David** is now widely regarded as the symbol for Sarasota.*

Lamb Shish Kebabs

Preparation time: 30 minutes   Serves 8
Marinating time: 6 hours
Broiling time: 10 - 15 minutes

2	pound leg of lamb, cut into 1" cubes
	salt and pepper to taste
	juice of 1 lemon
	juice of 1 orange
1	teaspoon oregano
1	cup olive oil
1	cup red wine
1	clove garlic, minced
16	small white onions, peeled
1	large green pepper, cut into 16 pieces

Combine meat with all ingredients except onions and peppers. Place in an earthenware bowl and marinate about 6 hours in the refrigerator, turning and stirring occasionally.

Preheat oven to broil.

Parboil onions for 3 minutes.

Drain meat and alternate on skewers with onions and green peppers. Broil 10 - 15 minutes turning occasionally.

Delicious with a garden salad and crusty bread on a hot summer evening.

Fine old frames adorn the paintings in the Ringling Museum. As John Ringling acquired works of art, he also collected unusually splendid frames, procured throughout Europe and in New York. These graceful windows on Ringling's world add greatly to the appearance and enjoyment of the Museum.

Veal Marsala

Preparation time: 30 minutes
Cooking time: 45 minutes

Serves 4

1½	pounds veal scallops
3	tablespoons flour
2	tablespoons oil
2	tablespoons butter or margarine
⅔	cup Marsala wine
⅓	cup fresh parsley, chopped
	salt and pepper to taste

Place scallops between sheets of waxed paper and pound paper thin with a meat cleaver. Dust with flour. Melt butter and oil together and brown scallops quickly. Cover with half the wine and cook, turning once, until wine is reduced and meat is tender. Remove to platter and keep warm.

Add remaining wine to pan. Bring to boil and add parsley. Pour over meat. Serve hot over white rice.

Veal Italiano

Preparation time: 45 minutes
Cooking time: 25 minutes

Serves 4

1	pound veal cutlets, cut into ½" strips	¼	teaspoon basil
⅓	cup olive oil	½	teaspoon oregano
2	cloves garlic, minced	2	tablespoons tomato paste
1	medium onion, finely chopped		salt and pepper to taste
1	16-ounce can whole tomatoes, chopped	½	cup freshly grated Parmesan cheese

Brown veal in hot oil over high heat. Remove from pan. Sauté onions and garlic until soft. Add remaining ingredients except cheese and simmer for 10 minutes. Add veal and cook over medium heat for 15 minutes or until tender.

To serve, top with freshly grated Parmesan cheese. Serve immediately over hot, cooked spaghetti.

Veal à la Marengo

Preparation time: 1 hour
Cooking time: 1½ hours

Serves 10 - 12

4	pounds lean veal, cut in 2" cubes
½	cup flour
	salt and pepper to taste
¼	cup olive oil
1	very large onion, chopped
1	cup dry white wine
1	cup chicken stock
2	cups canned Roma tomatoes, chopped
3	cloves garlic, minced
½	teaspoon tarragon
1	teaspoon thyme
2	tablespoons orange zest
¾	pound small, fresh mushrooms
½	cup fresh parsley, chopped

Mix flour with salt and pepper and dust veal cubes. Heat oil in Dutch oven over medium high setting and brown veal.

Remove veal. Add onions and sauté until limp. Add wine and chicken stock.

Return veal to pot. Add tomatoes, garlic, tarragon, thyme and orange zest.

Simmer, uncovered, for about 1¼ hours or until meat is very tender. Add mushrooms and simmer for another 15 minutes. Taste for seasoning.

Serve over hot noodles and garnish with a sprinkling of chopped parsley.

Veal Piccata Parmesan

Preparation time: 40 minutes
Cooking time: 15 minutes

Serves 6

2½	**pounds veal (20 medallions)**
½	**cup butter or margarine**
½	**cup lemon juice**
	garlic powder to taste
	paprika as needed
½ - ¾	**cup Parmesan cheese, freshly grated**
1	**large lemon, sliced thin**

Place veal between sheets of waxed paper and pound paper thin with a meat cleaver.

In large skillet, in melted butter to which lemon juice has been added, sauté veal for 4 minutes or until tender.

Remove veal from skillet and reserve pan liquid.

Spread veal on broiler pan which has been covered with foil. Sprinkle each piece with garlic powder and paprika. Cover with grated cheese. Top with a slice of lemon. Spoon pan liquid over each medallion and broil for 1 - 2 minutes, or just until cheese melts.

Serve immediately.

———•◦●◦•———

 Mable Ringling's wishes for a traditional formal Italian garden greatly influenced the design of the courtyard at the Ringling Museum. With graceful arches and more than 90 columns, the two long wings of the U-shaped Museum surround three descending balustraded terraces. Ancient Greek, Roman and Hellenistic statues and fountains, reproduced in cast stone, marble and bronze, adorn the gardens.

———•◦●◦•———

Curried Fruit Garnish

Preparation time: 15 minutes
Cooking time: 30 minutes

Serves 8 - 10

½	cup butter or margarine
2 - 3	teaspoons curry powder
1	cup brown sugar
1	29-ounce can each pear and peach halves, drained
1	20-ounce can pineapple slices, drained
1	16-ounce can apricot halves, drained

Preheat oven to 350°.

Melt butter, curry and sugar in small saucepan over medium heat. Place fruit in casserole dish. Pour butter mixture over fruit. Bake ½ hour. Refrigerate until ready to serve. Reheat before serving.

An excellent accompaniment to ham, chicken and pork.

Pickled Peach Garnish

Preparation time: 15 minutes
Cooking time: 10 minutes
Refrigeration time: 12 - 24 hours

Serves 8

2	29-ounce cans peach halves
¾	cup brown sugar
2	4" cinnamon sticks
1	teaspoon whole cloves
½	cup cider vinegar

Reserve juice from 1 can of peaches. Thoroughly drain peaches from other can. Combine juice, sugar, cinnamon sticks, cloves and vinegar. Boil 5 minutes. Add peaches and boil another 5 minutes, no longer. Refrigerate peaches in the syrup for 12 - 24 hours.

A tasty, tart accompaniment to meat, fish and poultry.

Poultry & Seafood

Coquina Chicken with Crabmeat

Preparation time: 45 minutes
Cooking time: 50 - 60 minutes

Serves 6

½	cup milk
½	cup chicken broth
½	cup dry white wine
¼	cup butter or margarine
½	cup mushrooms, chopped
¼	cup green onions, thinly sliced
3	tablespoons flour
7½	ounces crabmeat, if canned, well drained
¼	cup parsley, chopped
½	cup dry bread crumbs
¼	teaspoon salt
¼	teaspoon pepper
3	skinless, boneless chicken breasts, split, pounded thin
1	cup shredded Swiss cheese

Combine milk, broth and wine in a large cup.

In medium skillet over medium high heat melt 2 tablespoons butter. Sauté mushrooms and onions until golden. Set aside. In same skillet melt remaining butter over medium heat. Add flour and cook, stirring until blended, about 1 minute. Slowly blend in milk mixture, reserving ½ cup for later use. Cook and stir until smooth and slightly thickened, about 5 - 6 minutes. Remove from heat.

Preheat oven to 375°.

Combine crabmeat, parsley, bread crumbs, salt and pepper in a large bowl. Stir in ¼ cup of reserved milk mixture to create bread crumb mixture. Divide bread crumb mixture equally onto the chicken breasts. Roll chicken around mixture and secure with toothpicks. Arrange chicken breasts seam side down in lightly greased 9" x 13" baking dish. Pour remaining milk mixture over chicken and sprinkle with cheese.

Cover and bake 50 - 60 minutes, until golden brown.

Cornish Game Hens With Brown Rice

Preparation time: 20 minutes

Cooking time: 1 hour

Serves 4

Cornish Hens

4	Cornish game hens
2	cups cooked brown rice
1	teaspoon sugar
¾	teaspoon salt
⅛	teaspoon pepper
⅛	teaspoon nutmeg
⅛	teaspoon allspice

Sauce

3	tablespoons melted butter or margarine
½	cup red wine
2	tablespoons lemon juice

Preheat oven to 325°.

Wash hens and pat dry, inside and out. In a bowl, combine cooked rice, sugar, salt, pepper, nutmeg and allspice. Stuff hens with mixture. Place hens in a roasting pan. Bake 1 hour or until hens are tender.

Combine sauce ingredients and baste hens occasionally during baking.

———•·•●•·•———

 Upon John Ringling's death in 1936, his beloved Sarasota and the State of Florida became the beneficiaries of his Museum and its collections. By the terms of his will, the Museum's name may never be changed and it must remain in Sarasota. Nothing may be sold, traded or disposed of from the collection. Today, Sarasota owes its unique cultural distinction to this enduring, generous gift from John and Mable Ringling.

———•·•●•·•———

Opera House Baked Chicken in Sherry Sauce

Preparation time: 30 minutes
Cooking time: 45 - 60 minutes

Serves 6

2	tablespoons olive oil
3	whole skinless, boneless chicken breasts, split, rinsed, patted dry
¼	teaspoon each salt, pepper and basil
½	pint sour cream
1	can mushroom soup, undiluted
½	cup dry sherry
1	tablespoon each paprika and parsley

Preheat oven to 350°.

Heat oil over medium heat in large skillet. Add chicken breasts and brown each side. Remove to shallow baking dish and arrange chicken in a single layer. Sprinkle with salt, pepper and basil. In a small bowl, mix sour cream, mushroom soup and sherry. Pour over chicken. Bake uncovered for 45 - 60 minutes. Remove from oven. Sprinkle with paprika and parsley.

Apricot Chicken Cantonese

Preparation time: 30 minutes
Cooking time: 1½ hours

Serves 9

1	8 - 10 ounce bottle of Thousand Island dressing
1	package onion soup mix
1	8 - 10 ounce jar of apricot jam
2	whole chickens cut up

Preheat oven to 350°.

Combine dressing, soup mix and apricot jam in a large bowl. Lightly grease heavy duty roasting pan. Arrange chicken in a single layer. Spoon dressing mixture over chicken. Bake uncovered 1½ hours. Prick thigh or any large piece with tip of knife. If juices run clear, chicken has cooked through. If not, cook until done. Fat free dressing may be substituted.

Dijon Baked Chicken

Preparation time: 30 minutes
Cooking time: 1¼ hours

Serves 12

1½	**cups butter or margarine**
1	**clove of garlic, minced**
1	**tablespoon Dijon mustard**
1½	**teaspoons of Worcestershire sauce**
4½	**cups dried bread crumbs**
1¼	**cups grated Parmesan cheese**
1	**cup shredded cheddar cheese**
½	**teaspoon salt**
½	**cup chopped parsley**
12	**skinless, boneless chicken breasts, pounded thin**

Preheat oven to 350°.

Melt butter in shallow pan, add garlic, mustard and Worcestershire sauce and stir well. Let cool slightly. Combine bread crumbs, cheese, salt and parsley. Dip chicken in butter mixture and then in crumb mixture.

Roll breasts, secure with toothpicks and sprinkle with remaining crumbs. Place in shallow baking dish and drizzle remaining butter over chicken.

Bake 1¼ hours, basting occasionally.

— •●•• —

 One of the main attractions at The John and Mable Ringling Museum of Art is the collection of 17th-century baroque art. At the heart of this collection is the work of Peter Paul Rubens, one of the greatest artists of his time. Rubens' influence can be seen in the work of many Italian and Flemish painters represented in the Ringling collection.

— •●•• —

Renaissance Chicken with Wild Rice

Preparation time: 30 minutes   Serves 8
Cooking time: 1 hour

1	cup cooked wild rice
½	cup butter or margarine
½	cup onion, chopped
¼	cup flour
1	cup chicken broth
1	cup half-and-half or light cream
8	ounces fresh mushrooms, sautéed
3	cups cooked chicken, diced
1	teaspoon fresh parsley, minced
1½	teaspoons salt
¼	teaspoon pepper
½	teaspoon slivered almonds

Preheat oven to 350°.

Cook rice according to package directions and set aside.

Heat 1 tablespoon of butter over medium heat in a large skillet. Add onions and sauté until clear, about 3 - 4 minutes. Remove from heat.

Heat remaining butter in same skillet over medium heat. Stir in flour and blend. Cook about 2 minutes. Slowly whisk in chicken broth and cream and cook until mixture is smooth and slightly thickened. Add rice, onions, mushrooms, chicken, parsley, salt and pepper. Stir to blend. Add additional cream if needed to prevent over-thickening of sauce.

Spoon into lightly buttered 2-quart casserole dish. Sprinkle with almonds.

Bake about 1 hour, until hot and bubbly.

Desoto Chicken Divan

Preparation time: 20 minutes   Serves 8
Cooking time: 30 - 45 minutes

3	10-ounce packages frozen broccoli spears, defrosted
4	cooked boneless, skinless chicken breasts, cut in half
2	cans cream of chicken soup, undiluted
1	cup mayonnaise
1	teaspoon lemon juice
¼ - ½	teaspoon curry powder
¼	teaspoon salt
¼	teaspoon pepper
½	cup shredded sharp cheddar cheese
½	cup bread crumbs

Preheat oven to 350°.

Cook broccoli in salted water and drain. Arrange broccoli in lightly greased baking dish. Place chicken on top of broccoli.

Combine soup, mayonnaise, lemon juice, curry powder, salt and pepper in a large bowl. Pour over chicken. Sprinkle with cheese and bread crumbs.

Bake uncovered for 30 - 45 minutes, until hot and bubbly.

 When John Ringling acquired the large Peter Paul Rubens cartoons from the series **The Triumph of the Eucharist** *in 1926, he was in the planning stage of his art museum. He was therefore able to have a gallery designed especially to display these huge canvases. Today, the Rubens Gallery in the Ringling Museum epitomizes John Ringling's enthusiasm, intense energy and passion for achievement.*

Hawaiian Chicken

Preparation time: 45 minutes
Baking time: 1½ hours

Serves 6

¼	teaspoon paprika
2	teaspoons ginger
1½	cups flour
¼	teaspoon salt
¼	teaspoon pepper
1	3-pound chicken fryer, cut up
½	cup cooking oil
1	15-ounce can pineapple chunks
1	cup brown sugar
3	tablespoons soy sauce
1	teaspoon cider vinegar
1	medium green pepper, diced
1	medium onion, diced

Preheat oven to 325°.

Combine paprika, ginger, flour, salt and pepper in a plastic bag. Place chicken pieces in bag and shake until chicken is well coated.

Heat oil in large oven-proof skillet over medium high heat. Add chicken pieces one at a time. Cook, turning to brown evenly. Remove chicken. Drain on paper towel and reserve. Discard oil and clean the skillet for later use.

Strain pineapple over a bowl and set aside. Pour pineapple juice into a small sauce pan. Add brown sugar, soy sauce, vinegar, green pepper and onion. Heat to boil and remove from heat.

Arrange chicken pieces in skillet in a single layer. Pour pineapple juice mixture over chicken and evenly distribute pineapple pieces.

Bake covered 1 hour. Remove cover and bake for another ½ hour. Check after 15 minutes, add water if dry and serve with remaining pineapple juice mixture.

Malaysian Chicken & Pear Stir Fry

Preparation time: 40 minutes   Serves 4 - 6
Cooking time: 30 minutes

¾	cup cold water	¼	cup sliced almonds
3	tablespoons frozen orange juice	2	tablespoons cooking oil
4	teaspoons soy sauce	1	cup fresh mushrooms, sliced
1	tablespoon cornstarch	2	medium red peppers, cut into strips
¼	teaspoon ground ginger	2	medium pears, cored and sliced
¼	teaspoon ground cinnamon	12	ounces boned chicken breasts, cut into 1" pieces
⅛	teaspoon ground red pepper	4 - 6	cups cooked rice

Combine cold water, orange juice, soy sauce, cornstarch, ginger, cinnamon and red pepper. Set aside.

In a large skillet or wok, toast almonds 1 minute and remove. Reserve.

Heat 1 tablespoon of oil in skillet or wok over medium heat. Add mushrooms, peppers and pears and cook until tender. Set aside.

Heat remaining oil. Add the chicken and sauté until cooked through, 2 - 3 minutes. Add sauce to chicken. Cook and stir until thick. Return vegetables to skillet and heat through, about 2 minutes.

Serve over hot rice and sprinkle with toasted almonds.

 *The most impressive work by Peter Paul Rubens at the Ringling Museum is the series, **The Triumph of the Eucharist**. John Ringling acquired four of the 11 oversized canvases which comprised the series, commissioned as patterns for tapestries by the Hapsburg Archduchess Isabella in 1625. A fifth was purchased by the Museum and installed in 1980. These tapestry patterns, or "cartoons" as they are called, present Rubens' genius for powerful realism and his impassioned reaffirmation of Catholic religious beliefs.*

South Florida Hot Chicken Salad

Preparation time: 25 minutes   Serves 6
Cooking time: 40 - 45 minutes

2	cups cooked chicken, cubed
1	cup celery, diced
3	tablespoons pimiento, diced
2	tablespoons onion, chopped
1	teaspoon salt
½	teaspoon pepper
½	cup pitted black olives, sliced
½	cup slivered almonds
1	4-ounce can sliced water chestnuts, drained
⅔	cup mayonnaise
1	tablespoon lemon juice
2	cups crushed potato chips
½	cup shredded cheddar cheese

Preheat oven to 350°.

Combine chicken, celery, pimiento, onion, salt, pepper, olives, almonds and water chestnuts in a large bowl.

In a small bowl, mix mayonnaise and lemon juice. Blend into chicken mixture.

Lightly grease a 2-quart casserole dish. Spoon mixture into dish and sprinkle with potato chips and cheese.

Bake 40 - 45 minutes, until hot and bubbly.

Bombay Chicken Curry

Preparation time: 15 minutes   Serves 8
Cooking time: 1 - 1¼ hours

¼	cup butter or margarine
½	cup honey
¼	cup Dijon mustard
2	tablespoons prepared mustard
1	tablespoon curry
½	teaspoon lime juice
1	teaspoon grated lime peel
1	teaspoon salt
1	clove garlic, minced
8	skinless, boneless chicken breasts
8	cups cooked rice

Preheat oven to 350°.

Combine all of the ingredients except the chicken breasts and the rice in a medium sauce pan. Whisk to blend and bring to a boil. Boil 2 minutes, stirring constantly. Remove from heat and set aside.

Place the chicken breasts in a lightly greased 9" x 13" baking dish. Pour sauce over chicken. Bake uncovered 1 - 1¼ hours, depending on the size of the breasts.

Serve over hot rice.

—••●••—

*Abraham and Melchizedek is one of the most dramatic scenes from Peter Paul Rubens' series **The Triumph of the Eucharist** in The John and Mable Ringling Museum of Art. Rubens, a devout man of faith, used focused light, brilliant color and converging energy to rivet attention on this ancient biblical drama surrounded by an illusory architectural framework.*

—••●••—

Shanghai Chicken Chow Mein

Preparation time: 30 minutes   Serves 6
Cooking time: 20 minutes

2	tablespoons butter or margarine
1	medium onion, chopped
1	4.5 ounce jar whole button mushrooms, drained
1	cup celery, cut diagonally in ½" pieces
1½	cups chicken broth
2	tablespoons soy sauce
1	tablespoon sugar
1½	tablespoons corn starch
3	tablespoons cold water
1	4-ounce can bamboo shoots, drained
1½	cups cooked chicken, cubed (1 - 2 pieces)
1	6-ounce bag chow mein noodles

Heat butter in large skillet over high heat. Lightly brown onions and mushrooms. Add celery, chicken broth, soy sauce and sugar. Reduce heat to low and simmer for 10 minutes. Blend corn starch and water into chicken broth mixture. Cook, stirring until clear and thick. Stir in bamboo shoots and chicken. Cook until heated through, about 1 - 2 minutes. remove from heat.

Spoon over chow mein noodles. Serve with orange sherbet, macaroons and hot tea.

———————————•••••———————————

 One of the magnificent portraits found in the Ringling Museum is the 1635 ***Portrait of the Archduke Ferdinand*** *by Peter Paul Rubens. Brother of Spain's King Phillip IV and christened "Defender of the Faith," Ferdinand led the Catholic Counter-Reformation in northwestern Europe. Respected by family, countrymen and the Pope, Ferdinand embodied the values of the devoutly religious Rubens, who honored the Archduke with this state portrait.*

———————————•••••———————————

Anna María Lemon Basil Fish

Preparation time: 10 minutes   Serves 8
Cooking time: 15 - 20 minutes (snapper, walleyed pike), 45 minutes (trout, white fish)

4	**pounds of snapper, walleyed pike, trout, or white fish, well rinsed**
½	**cup butter or margarine, melted**
3	**tablespoons lemon juice**
3	**tablespoons fresh basil, chopped**
½	**teaspoon each salt, pepper and paprika**
dash	**lemon pepper (optional)**
1	**tablespoon parsley, chopped**
1	**lemon, thinly sliced**

Preheat oven to 375°.

Arrange fish in a 9" x 13" baking pan and cover with melted butter and lemon juice. Sprinkle with basil, salt, pepper, paprika and lemon pepper. Bake fish, basting frequently, about 45 minutes or until it flakes easily with tip of knife. Garnish with parsley and lemon slices and serve.

Broiled White Fish with Anchovy Sauce

Preparation time: 10 minutes   Serves 4
Cooking time: 7 - 10 minutes

2	**cloves garlic, minced**
⅛	**cup olive oil**
2	**rounded tablespoons anchovy paste**
2	**tablespoons parsley, chopped**
1	**teaspoon lemon juice**
1	**pound white fish, cut into four fillets, well rinsed**

In small saucepan over medium heat, cook garlic in oil until golden. Stir in anchovy paste, parsley and lemon juice until blended. Set aside. Heat oven to broil. Arrange fish in a lightly greased broiling pan. Brush sauce over each fillet and sprinkle with pepper to taste. Broil 7 - 10 minutes until fish flakes easily with tip of knife. Cook fish 10 minutes for each 1" thickness of fillet.

Turtle Beach Baked Salmon with Herbed Butter

Preparation time: 15 minutes
Cooking time: 10 minutes

Serves 4

4	salmon steaks, 1" thick
1	stick butter or margarine, 4 tablespoons melted
3	teaspoons lemon juice
¼	teaspoon salt
¼	teaspoon pepper
1	tablespoon parsley, fresh rosemary, or tarragon
1	lemon, thinly sliced
dash	paprika

Preheat oven to 350°.

Arrange fish in single layer in baking dish. Drizzle with 4 tablespoons melted butter, lemon juice, salt and pepper. Cover dish with lid or foil. Bake 10 minutes or until fish flakes easily. Uncover and remove to heated platter.

Meanwhile, heat remaining butter and herbs in small saucepan. Sauté 1 - 2 minutes over low heat. Spoon butter-herb mixture over salmon. Garnish with lemon slices and dust with paprika.

This recipe can also be used with cod or turbot.

—•••••—

 *Since becoming the State Art Museum of Florida in 1936, The John and Mable Ringling Museum of Art has acquired several important works that echo John and Mable Ringling's artistic tastes and interests. American Robert Henri's 1909 **Salome** is one such work, with the dramatic, dark background and painterly strokes reminiscent of baroque art. One of Henri's greatest works, its seductive, exotic dance captures the sort of daring movement and energy for which the Ringlings showed such affection.*

—•••••—

Sanibel Salmon with Dill Sauce

Preparation time: 30 minutes
Cooking time: 10 minutes
Refrigeration time: 2 hours

Serves 6

Dill Sauce

1	large egg
1	teaspoon each salt and sugar
¼	teaspoon pepper
4	teaspoons lemon juice
1	teaspoon onion, grated
2	tablespoons dill, finely chopped
1½	cups sour cream

Salmon Mold

1	tablespoon gelatin
¼	cup water or white wine
1	tablespoon butter or margarine
3	tablespoons shallots, chopped fine
1½	cups fish stock
1¼	pounds cooked or drained canned salmon
2	tablespoons brandy
½	teaspoon salt
⅛	teaspoon each pepper and paprika
½	cup whipping cream
1	lemon, sliced
1	tablespoon capers, washed and drained

For dill sauce, beat ingredients together in bowl. Set aside and chill. In a small bowl, soften gelatin in water or wine. In a large saucepan, sauté shallots in butter over medium heat. Add fish stock and softened gelatin. Heat until gelatin dissolves. You may substitute a half bottle of clam juice and ⅛ cup water for the stock. In a blender, put some of the stock and some of the salmon. Puree all of the salmon in small quantities. When salmon is pureed, add brandy, salt, pepper and paprika. Fold in cream. Spoon mixture into a buttered mold and chill until it sets. To serve, unmold onto a serving platter. Surround with lemon slices, watercress leaves and capers. Serve with dill sauce on the side.

Okeechobee Flounder & Vegetable Dijon

Preparation time: 30 minutes
Cooking time: 20 minutes

Serves 4

¾	**cup milk**
1½	**teaspoons cornstarch**
1½	**teaspoons Dijon mustard**
1	**teaspoon chicken bouillon granules**
1	**tablespoon butter or margarine**
½	**cup fresh mushrooms, thinly sliced**
⅓	**cup zucchini, thinly sliced**
¼	**cup carrots, cut in 1" strips**
¼	**cup green onions, sliced**
4	**fillets of flounder, 3 - 4 ounces each**
1	**tablespoon fresh parsley, chopped**

Preheat oven to 450°.

Whisk milk, cornstarch, mustard and chicken granules together in a small bowl. Set aside. In medium skillet over medium heat, melt butter. Add mushrooms, zucchini, carrots and onions. Sauté about 2 minutes.

In lightly greased baking dish, bake fish 5 minutes for each ½" of thickness or until fish flakes easily with tip of fork. Meanwhile, add milk mixture to vegetables. Reduce heat to medium low. Cook, stirring until mixture thickens slightly. Remove from heat. Arrange cooked fish on serving platter. Pour sauce over fillets, sprinkle with parsley and serve.

—•••—

 *Of great merit and significance in John Ringling's collection of over 50 Dutch paintings from the 17th century is **Still Life with Parrots** by Jan Davidsz. de Heem. This work exhibits both the exquisite attention to detail characteristic of Dutch works of the period, and the lavish, resplendent manner of 17th-century Flemish painting. The composition uses a cascade of color to give the painting unity.*

—•••—

Islandside Poached Salmon with Ginger-Mustard Sauce

Preparation time: 30 minutes
Cooking time: 10 minutes

Serves 6

Sauce

2	tablespoons tarragon vinegar
2	tablespoons Dijon mustard
½	cup olive oil
2	tablespoons onion, minced
1	tablespoon fresh ginger, grated
	teaspoon garlic, minced

Poached Salmon

6	salmon fillets, 6" x 1" thick, well rinsed
1	cup water
10	large sprigs fresh dill
10	whole black peppercorns
6	whole garlic cloves, smashed
3	tablespoons white vinegar
2	bay leaves
¼	teaspoon salt

Garnish

fresh dill sprigs to taste
diced pimiento to taste

To make ginger-mustard sauce, put vinegar and mustard in a small bowl. Whisk in olive oil and blend well. Whisk in onion, ginger and garlic. Set aside. This sauce can be made a day ahead and refrigerated. Heat before serving with fish.

To cook fish, place fillets in large skillet and cover with water. Add dill, peppercorns, garlic, vinegar, bay leaves and salt. Cover skillet with tightly fitting lid. Bring water to boil. Reduce heat to medium. Simmer about 5 minutes. Be careful not to over cook.

Remove fish with slatted spoon to heated platter. Spoon heated sauce over fish. Sprinkle with fresh dill and pimiento and serve.

West Coast Salmon with Cucumber Sauce

Preparation time: 30 minutes   Serves 4
Refrigeration time: 3 hours

Sauce

2	large cucumbers, halved lengthwise, seeded, thinly sliced
½	cup mayonnaise
½	cup sour cream or yogurt
1	teaspoon fresh dill, chopped
½	teaspoon salt
½	teaspoon pepper

Salmon

4	salmon steaks, 1" thick
4	tablespoons butter or margarine, melted
3	teaspoons lemon juice
¼	teaspoon salt
¼	teaspoon pepper

Arrange sliced cucumbers on paper towel, sprinkle with salt and let stand about 30 minutes to drain. Then combine cucumbers with remaining sauce ingredients. Cover. Refrigerate to chill several hours.

Use melon baller or tip of teaspoon to remove cucumber seeds. Cucumbers will keep 1 - 2 days if refrigerated. If water accumulates on top, blot with paper towel.

Preheat oven to 350°.

Arrange fish in single layer in baking dish. Drizzle with melted butter, lemon juice, salt and pepper. Cover the dish with a lid or foil. Bake 10 minutes or until fish flakes easily. Uncover and remove to heated platter.

Pour cucumber sauce over fish and serve.

Orange-Soy Marinated Fish

Preparation time: 10 minutes   Serves 4
Marinating time: 2 hours or more
Cooking time: 10 minutes for fish 1" thick

⅓	cup orange juice
⅓	cup soy sauce
2	tablespoons olive oil
1	clove garlic, minced
½	teaspoon basil
1½	pounds salmon, tuna, or swordfish, 1" thick, well rinsed

Heat oven to broil.

For marinade, combine all ingredients except fish in a large bowl.

Arrange fish in a large shallow baking dish. Pour marinade over fish, turning once or twice to coat. Cover. Refrigerate for several hours, turning several times.

Drain fish from marinade. Arrange on lightly greased broiler pan. Place on top oven rack. Broil 10 minutes or until fish flakes easily with tip of knife.

Remove to serving platter. Garnish as desired.

––––––––––– •●•• –––––––––––

Among the Ringling Museum's 19th-century American works is the 1885 painting **Still Life with Oranges** *by Alfred F. King. This study artfully demonstrates a kind of painting popular with American artists at the turn of the century, trompe l'oeil. The brush strokes are invisible and the fruit is portrayed life-size. With a fascination for shiny surfaces and sensual textures, the artist recreates the brilliant color and tiny imperfections of the oranges.*

––––––––––– •●•• –––––––––––

Red Snapper Cà d'Zan

Preparation time: 25 minutes

Baking time: 30 minutes

2	pounds red snapper fillets, well rinsed
½	teaspoon salt
½	teaspoon pepper
3	tablespoons butter or margarine
1	medium onion, chopped
2	green onions, chopped
1	garlic clove, minced
1½	tablespoons flour
½	cup dry white wine
4	tomatoes, peeled, seeded and chopped
1	teaspoon parsley, chopped
½	teaspoon basil
½	teaspoon thyme
¼	cup fine bread crumbs
3	tablespoons Parmesan cheese, freshly grated

Preheated oven 350°.

Arrange fillets in single layer in lightly buttered baking dish. Sprinkle with salt and pepper.

Melt butter in small saucepan over medium heat. Add onions and garlic. Sauté until limp, about 5 minutes. Stir in flour, cooking 5 minutes until mixture is blended. Slowly whisk in wine. Heat to boil, then simmer 5 minutes until lightly thickened. Stir in tomatoes, herbs, salt and pepper. Pour sauce over fillets. Sprinkle with bread crumbs and Parmesan cheese.

Bake uncovered about 30 minutes, or until fish flakes easily with tip of knife.

Broiled Marinated Swordfish with Angel Hair Pasta

Preparation time: 10 minutes
Marinating time: 3 hours
Cooking time: 10 minutes

Serves 4

Marinade

½	cup soy sauce
½	cup strong tea
½	cup sherry
½	teaspoon cinnamon
½	teaspoon pepper
¼	teaspoon oregano
¼	teaspoon cloves
1	clove garlic, minced

Swordfish

4	6-ounce swordfish steaks, well rinsed
3	tablespoons fresh cilantro, chopped
½	pound angel hair pasta, cooked and buttered

Mix marinade ingredients to blend in a large bowl. Arrange fish in a large shallow baking dish. Pour marinade over fish, turning once or twice to coat. Cover. Refrigerate for several hours, turning several times.

Heat oven to broil.

Remove fish from marinade to broiling pan. Place on top oven rack. Broil 10 minutes or until fish flakes easily with tip of knife.

Remove fish to heated platter and sprinkle with cilantro. Serve with buttered angel hair pasta.

Longboat Key Crab Cakes

Preparation time: 30 minutes
Cooking time: 10 minutes

Serves 2 - 4

1	**pound white crabmeat**
1	**cup green onions, finely chopped**
1½	**cups bread crumbs**
2	**large eggs**
¼	**cup milk**
1	**teaspoon Worcestershire sauce**
½	**teaspoon salt**
¼	**teaspoon pepper**
1	**tablespoon Dijon mustard**
¼	**cup oil**

Mix crab, onions and ¾ cup of the bread crumbs.

In separate bowl, beat eggs. Add milk, Worcestershire sauce, salt, pepper and mustard. Pour over crab mixture and mix. Shape into ½" thick patties and dip into remaining crumbs to coat well.

Heat oil in large skillet to medium high. Fry cakes about 5 minutes on each side until golden.

Drain on paper towels and serve.

––––––––––••●•••••––––––––––

 Among the Ringling Museum's treasures on permanent display is a collection of nearly 200 Western European and Chinese fans dating from the 18th to 20th centuries. Decorated mainly with romantic scenes, many of the fans have historical significance. One fan, adorned by ostrich feathers and a silver handle, is one of only 25 replicas of the original carried by Princess Diana at her royal wedding.

––––––––––••●•••••––––––––––

Gasparilla Baked Crab & Shrimp

Preparation time: 20 minutes   Serves 6
Cooking time: 30 - 40 minutes

Crab
1	13-ounce can flaked crabmeat
6 - 8	ounce can large shrimp
1	medium onion, chopped fine
1	small green pepper, finely chopped
1	cup celery, finely chopped
1	cup mayonnaise
1	teaspoon Worcestershire sauce
1	teaspoon lemon juice
¼	teaspoon salt
¼	teaspoon pepper

Topping
1	cup buttered crumbs
3	tablespoons fresh parsley, finely chopped

Preheat oven to 350°.

In medium bowl, mix ingredients until well blended. Spoon mixture into baking shells or ramekins, dividing evenly. Arrange on shallow baking pan. Sprinkle with bread crumbs.

Bake 30 - 40 minutes, until hot and bubbly. Remove. Sprinkle with fresh parsley and serve.

If canned crabmeat is used, drain well. If frozen crabmeat is used, defrost and squeeze out all excess water.

Key Largo Shrimp Artichoke Casserole

Preparation time: 30 minutes
Cooking time: 30 minutes

Serves 4 - 6

4	tablespoons butter or margarine
2½	tablespoons flour
½	teaspoon salt
¼	teaspoon pepper
1	cup half-and-half cream
1	tablespoon Worcestershire sauce
¼	cup dry sherry
1	pound shrimp, cooked
1	can whole artichokes, drained
½	pound fresh mushrooms, sautéed
¼	cup Parmesan cheese
½	teaspoon paprika
2	tablespoons parsley, finely chopped

Preheat oven to 375°.

Melt butter in sauce pan over medium heat. Add flour, cook 5 minutes, whisking to blend. Add salt, pepper, half-and-half, Worcestershire sauce and sherry. Cook and blend until mixture is smooth and slightly thickened. Set aside.

Arrange shrimp, artichoke hearts and mushrooms in layers in lightly greased 2-quart casserole dish. Pour the sauce on top. Sprinkle with Parmesan cheese and paprika.

Bake 30 minutes or until hot and bubbly.

Garnish with parsley. Can be served over rice, with a green salad, french bread, white wine and a chocolate angel food cake for dessert.

St. Armands Crabmeat Casserole

Preparation time: 20 minutes   Serves 6 - 8
Cooking time: 30 minutes

4	tablespoons butter or margarine, melted
2	tablespoons flour
1	cup milk
3	boxes frozen crabmeat, defrosted, rinsed, drained
2	teaspoon lemon juice
1	teaspoon mustard
½	teaspoon horseradish
1	teaspoon salt
3	hard boiled eggs, finely chopped
1	tablespoon parsley, finely chopped

Preheat oven to 350°.

In small saucepan, melt butter. Blend in flour and slowly add milk, stirring constantly until thickened and smooth. Set aside.

In an ovenproof casserole dish, combine remaining ingredients. Mix to blend. Pour white sauce over crab mixture. Mix to blend well.

Bake 30 minutes or until hot and bubbly.

The main entrance to The John and Mable Ringling Museum of Art features elegant doors that once opened into the residence of New York society's Mrs. William Astor. When the Astor mansion and its contents were auctioned in New York in 1926, John Ringling purchased many of its distinguished architectural details and incorporated them into his Museum. Among his acquisitions installed in the Museum's galleries were two complete rooms which were reproductions of 18th-century French salons.

Bay Point Shrimp Casserole

Preparation time: 30 minutes   Serves 8
Cooking time: 20 - 30 minutes

3	**pounds shrimp, shelled, deveined**
2	**tablespoons butter or margarine**
1	**minced onion**
½	**pound mushrooms, sliced**
2	**tomatoes, diced**
2	**tablespoons flour**
½	**cup half-and-half cream**
¼	**cup sherry**
1	**tablespoon Worcestershire sauce**
¼	**teaspoon salt**
¼	**teaspoon pepper**
¼	**teaspoon paprika**
½	**cup buttered bread crumbs**

Preheat oven to 350°.

To cook shrimp, heat water to boil over high heat. Add shrimp. Reduce heat to medium. Cook shrimp 3 minutes or until they turn pink. Drain. Run under cold water to stop cooking. Pat dry on paper towels.

Lightly grease 2-quart casserole dish.

In medium saucepan over medium heat, melt ½ tablespoon butter. Add onion. Cook until limp, about 3 minutes. Set aside. In same saucepan, melt ½ tablespoon butter. Add mushrooms and tomatoes. Cook until lightly browned, about 5 minutes. Remove and add to onions.

In same saucepan, melt remaining butter. Add flour. Cook, whisking to blend, about 3 minutes. Do not brown. Slowly add cream, whisking to blend. Cook until slightly thickened and smooth. Add sherry, Worcestershire sauce, salt, pepper and paprika, stir to blend. Remove from heat.

Stir in cooked shrimp. Pour into large buttered casserole dish. Sprinkle with bread crumbs. Bake 30 minutes, until top has lightly browned and mixture is hot.

Shrimp de Jonghe

Preparation time: 20 minutes
Cooking time: 15 minutes

Serves 6

2	pounds of shrimp, shelled, deveined	1	tablespoon green onion, chopped
½	cup butter or margarine	2	tablespoons chives, chopped
1	clove of garlic, chopped	2	tablespoons parsley, chopped
½	cup bread crumbs, from french bread		salt to taste
½	cup dry sherry		pinch of cayenne pepper

Preheat oven to 350°.

Add shrimp to boiling water. Reduce heat to medium. Cook shrimp 3 minutes or until they turn pink. Drain. Immerse in cold water to stop cooking. Pat dry on paper towels. Place shrimp in baking shells or ramekins. Melt butter in small saucepan over medium heat. Add garlic. Cook 2 minutes. Do not brown garlic. Remove from heat, add remaining ingredients. Toss well and spoon over shrimp. Bake 15 minutes or until brown.

Sea Island Scalloped Oysters

Preparation time: 10 minutes
Cooking time: 20 - 25 minutes

Serves 3

1	stick butter or margarine	½	teaspoon salt
3	tablespoons shallots, chopped	⅛	teaspoon pepper
1½	cup cracker crumbs	1	cup medium cream
1	pint oysters, drained		

Preheat oven to 375°.

Lightly butter a shallow 1-quart baking dish. In a small skillet over medium heat, sauté shallots in 1 tablespoon of butter. In medium bowl, toss cracker crumbs, remaining butter and shallots to blend. Spread half the crumbs in a greased baking dish. Arrange oysters over crumbs and sprinkle with salt and pepper. Pour cream on oysters and top with remaining crumbs. Bake until crumbs are nicely browned, 20 - 25 minutes. Remove and serve.

Shrimp Newburg

Preparation time: 40 minutes
Cooking time: 20 minutes

Serves 6

2	**pounds shrimp**
4	**tablespoons butter or margarine**
4	**tablespoons flour**
2	**cups cream**
6	**tablespoons catsup**
1½	**tablespoons Worcestershire sauce**
¼	**teaspoon salt**
¼	**teaspoon paprika**
¼	**teaspoon cayenne pepper**
3	**tablespoons sherry**
1	**tablespoon parsley**
6	**cups cooked rice**

To cook shrimp, heat water to boil over high heat. Add shrimp. Reduce heat to medium. Cook shrimp 3 minutes or until they turn pink. Drain. Immerse in cold water to stop cooking. Pat dry on paper towels.

In medium saucepan over medium heat, melt butter. Add flour and whisk to blend. Cook 5 minutes. Do not brown flour. Reduce heat to medium low. Slowly add cream, whisking to blend.

Cook until smooth and slightly thickened. Whisk in catsup, Worcestershire sauce, salt, paprika and cayenne pepper. Add sherry and cooked shrimp. Reheat 1 minute.

Garnish with parsley. Serve over white rice.

———————————•••••———————————

 The John and Mable Ringling Museum of Art houses America's largest collection of archaic and classical antiquities from Cyprus—over 1,000 pieces—outside of New York's Metropolitan Museum of Art.

———————————•••••———————————

Boca Grande Shrimp Curry

Preparation time: 30 minutes
Cooking time: 30 minutes

Serves 8

3	pounds shrimp
½	cup minced onion
5	tablespoons butter or margarine
6	tablespoons flour
1	cup chicken broth
2	cups milk
1½	teaspoons sugar
3	teaspoons to 3 tablespoons curry powder, to taste
¼	teaspoon salt
1	teaspoon lemon juice
8	cups cooked rice

Accompaniments

chopped avocado, crumbled bacon
chutney, sieved hard-boiled eggs
chopped onions, chopped peanuts
raisins, toasted coconut

To cook shrimp, heat water to boil over high heat. Add shrimp. Reduce heat to medium. Cook shrimp 3 minutes or until they turn pink. Drain. Immerse in cold water to stop cooking. Pat dry on paper towels.

In medium saucepan, cook onion in butter over medium heat, until golden. Blend in flour, cook 5 minutes. Whisk in broth and milk.

Cook until smooth and thickened. Add sugar, curry powder and salt. Add shrimp and lemon juice. Reheat 1 minute.

Serve over hot rice. Put the accompaniments in separate bowls to be used for toppings on the curried shrimp.

Coquille St. Jacques

Preparation time: 30 minutes
Cooking time: 10 minutes

Serves 6

1½	**pounds scallops, coarsely chopped**
½	**cup dry white wine**
½	**teaspoon salt**
dash	**cayenne pepper**
2	**tablespoons shallots or green onions, finely chopped**
3	**tablespoons butter or margarine**
3	**tablespoons flour**
½	**cup heavy cream**
1	**cup sharp cheddar cheese, grated**
½	**cup buttered soft bread crumbs**

Preheat oven to 400°.

Place scallops in medium saucepan. Add wine, salt, cayenne and shallots. Bring to a boil, cover, reduce heat to low and simmer 10 minutes. Drain, reserving 1 cup of the stock.

In same saucepan, melt butter over medium heat. Whisk in flour. Cook until mixture is well blended, about 5 minutes.

Slowly whisk in reserved stock and heavy cream. Cook, stirring until thickened. Stir in cheese and scallops. Cook and stir until mixture is blended and cheese has melted.

Put the mixture in a casserole dish, cover with bread crumbs and bake 10 minutes or until light brown.

 It is not surprising that John Ringling, art connoisseur and collector of the 1920s, held the 17th-century artist Peter Paul Rubens in such high admiration. Rubens epitomized the extroverted ideal of the baroque man. He was a master of illusion and theatricality.

Vegetables

Everglades Asparagus Vinaigrette

Preparation time: 10 minutes
Marinating time: 2 hours
Cooking time: 8 minutes

Serves 6 - 8

2	pounds asparagus
1	tablespoon onion, finely chopped
1	teaspoon salt
¼	teaspoon dry mustard
1	tablespoon dill pickle, finely chopped
2	tablespoons red wine vinegar
1	teaspoon lemon juice
¼	cup olive oil
1	tablespoon parsley, chopped
1	lemon (optional)

Steam asparagus about 8 minutes. Cool and refrigerate.

Combine remaining ingredients in cruet and shake well. Add parsley. Pour over asparagus and marinate for several hours.

Garnish with lemon slices, if desired.

—••●••—

 John and Mable Ringling's winter estate in Sarasota is among the great American homes built during the 1920s. Christened "Cà d'Zan," or "House of John" in Venetian dialect, it was designed by New York architect Dwight James Baum to be a palatial Italian villa. Baum's design accommodated the Ringlings' fascination with the colorful and ornate, found especially in Venetian architecture. The Cà d'Zan was for John a reflection of his success in his business and personal ambitions.

—••●••—

Boston Baked Beans

Preparation time: 10 minutes
Cooking time: 1½ hours

Serves 8

2	1-pound cans pork and beans	¼	cup molasses
¾	cup brown sugar	½	cup catsup
1	teaspoon dry mustard	1	large onion, chopped
1	teaspoon ginger	6	slices bacon, chopped
½	teaspoon pepper		

Preheat oven to 325°.

Combine all ingredients in a casserole dish. Mix gently but well. Bake uncovered for 1½ hours. Check to be sure it doesn't dry out, especially around the edges. Stir occasionally and add a little water if necessary.

Gourmet Baked Kidney Beans

Preparation time: 30 minutes
Cooking time: 2 - 3 hours

Serves 12 - 15

1	14-ounce bottle of catsup	2	green peppers, chopped
1½	teaspoons Tabasco Sauce	3	tomatoes, chopped
¼	teaspoon ground allspice	6	thick slices bacon, chopped
1	cup dark brown sugar, firmly packed	5	1-pound cans red kidney beans, drained
2	medium onions, chopped		

Preheat oven to 325°.

In a bowl combine catsup, Tabasco Sauce, allspice and brown sugar. Set aside. In a separate bowl, combine onions, green peppers and tomatoes and set aside.

Layer ingredients in a 9" x 13" baking dish. Place bacon in the bottom, cover with half the beans, spread onion mixture, cover with remaining beans and top with catsup mixture. Bake 2 - 3 hours until brown but not dry. Add water if necessary to prevent dryness.

Green Bean & Cheese Casserole

Preparation time: 30 minutes
Cooking time: 40 minutes

Serves 6 - 8

2	packages frozen green beans or 1½ pounds fresh green beans
4	tablespoons butter or margarine
½	cup cracker crumbs
2	tablespoons flour
1	cup sour cream
1½	teaspoons sugar
	salt and pepper to taste
¾	teaspoon onion, grated
¼	pound Swiss cheese, chopped into small pieces

Preheat oven to 325°.

Steam beans in vegetable steamer until tender.

Melt 2 tablespoons butter and combine with cracker crumbs. Set aside.

Melt remaining butter in a saucepan. Blend in flour, then add sour cream, sugar, salt, pepper and onion. Stir until thick. Add cheese and remove from heat instantly.

Mix beans with cheese sauce. Cover with buttered cracker crumbs and bake 40 minutes.

This dish is good with rare beef or chicken. Serve with an aspic and hard rolls, as this casserole is rich and filling.

———————•●•———————

A deliberately imposing, Moorish gate house greeted guests of the Cà d'Zan. Passing through the impressive iron gates in a steady stream, John and Mable Ringling's visitors were awe-struck by an enchanting 37 acres of rich, tropical foliage and the sea breezes. It was both a romantic setting for Mable's musicales and a dramatic stage for John's VIP dinners.

———————•●•———————

Sherried Broiled Tomatoes

Preparation time: 15 minutes
Cooking time: 6 minutes

Serves 4

4	large, ripe but firm tomatoes
¼	cup dry sherry
	salt and pepper to taste
1	teaspoon dried oregano
8	tablespoons mayonnaise
¼	cup fresh grated Parmesan cheese

Preheat oven to 300°.

Cut tomatoes in half. Place in shallow baking dish, cut side up. Prick with fork. Sprinkle with sherry and let rest briefly. Sprinkle with salt, pepper and oregano. Bake 5 minutes. Remove from oven. Top tomato halves with mayonnaise and dust with Parmesan cheese. Turn heat to broil. Broil until lightly browned. Serve immediately.

Creamy Broccoli Ring

Preparation time: 30 minutes
Cooking time: 30 - 40 minutes

Serves 6

2	cups frozen chopped broccoli	1	tablespoon butter or margarine, melted
1	cup mayonnaise	1	tablespoon flour
1	cup heavy cream or evaporated milk	½	teaspoon salt
3	large eggs	2	pounds fresh broccoli (optional)

Preheat oven to 350°.

Cook broccoli according to package directions and cool. Mix ingredients and pour into a buttered ring mold or baking dish. Set in pan of warm water and bake until firm on top, about 30 - 40 minutes.

Serving suggestion: after unmolding, steam fresh broccoli flowerettes and arrange in center of ring.

Harts Landing Apricot Glazed Carrots

Preparation time: 20 minutes
Cooking time: 20 minutes

Serves 6

2	pounds carrots, peeled, cut diagonally	1	teaspoon salt
3	tablespoons butter or margarine	1	teaspoon grated orange zest
⅓	cup apricot preserves	2	teaspoons fresh lemon juice
¼	teaspoon ground nutmeg		fresh parsley (optional)

Place carrots in a small amount of salted water in a saucepan. Cover saucepan, bring water to a boil, then lower heat and simmer until tender, about 20 minutes. Drain and set aside. Melt butter and stir in apricot preserves until blended. Add nutmeg, salt, orange zest and lemon juice. Toss carrots with apricot mixture. Garnish with parsley.

Stillwater Sweet & Sour Carrots

Preparation time: 30 minutes
Cooking time: 25 minutes

Serves 6 - 8

1	pound carrots, peeled and diagonally cut
1	small green pepper, seeded and cut into narrow strips
1	8-ounce can pineapple chunks, drained, reserve juice
⅓	cup sugar
1	teaspoon cornstarch
½	teaspoon salt
2	tablespoons vinegar
2	teaspoons soy sauce

Place carrots in a small amount of water in a saucepan. Cover saucepan, bring water to a boil then lower heat and simmer until tender, about 15 minutes. Add green pepper and simmer 3 minutes longer. Drain vegetables. Add pineapple chunks. Add water to pineapple juice if necessary to make ⅓ cup liquid. Combine sugar, cornstarch and salt in a saucepan. Stir in pineapple liquid, vinegar and soy sauce. Cook until thick, stirring continuously. Pour over vegetables.

This dish can be served hot or cold.

Cumberland Baked Red Cabbage

Preparation time: 30 minutes
Cooking time: 1¼ hours

Makes 2 quarts

1	head red cabbage, approximately 2½ pounds
4	tablespoons butter or margarine
1	medium onion, finely chopped
5	tablespoons brown sugar
1½	teaspoons salt
⅓	cup water
⅔	cup white vinegar
1	tart apple, peeled and thinly sliced
¼	cup red currant jelly

Preheat oven to 325°.

Wash cabbage in cold water. Cut in half, core and slice very fine.

Using a Dutch oven, melt the butter and brown the onion. Add sugar, salt, water, vinegar and apple and bring to a boil. Add cabbage and stir to coat. Bring to a second boil and cover tightly. Bake 1 hour 15 minutes. Stir occasionally and add water if necessary to prevent dryness. About 15 minutes before cabbage is done, mix in currant jelly.

The decoration and furnishing of the Ringling mansion, Cà d'Zan, were done by the Ringlings themselves, without the help of an interior decorator. In what was one of their favorite pursuits, they haunted the exclusive auction houses of Europe and New York, outfitting their home in treasures and reproductions from around the world.

Their 24 dining chairs covered in 18th-century embroidered red velvet once accommodated guests at the Vanderbilts' Newport home. Two 17th-century Flemish tapestries were purchased at auction from the home of New York City's Vincent Astor.

Festive Peas with Pimentos

Preparation time: 30 minutes
Cooking time: 20 minutes

Serves 4

1	cup celery, finely chopped
1	cup chicken stock
2	cups fresh peas
⅛	pound fresh mushrooms, sliced
¼	teaspoon salt (or to taste)
1	small jar of pimentos, drained and diced

Cook celery in chicken stock over moderate heat for 10 minutes. Add peas and mushrooms. Reduce heat. Simmer uncovered for 5 to 10 minutes, cooking until peas are just tender. Salt to taste. Garnish with diced pimento.

Stir-fry Pea Pods & Peppers

Preparation time: 45 minutes
Cooking time: 10 minutes

Serves 6

2	tablespoons each red wine vinegar and soy sauce
½	teaspoon sugar
2 - 3	tablespoons sesame oil
2	red bell peppers, seeded and slivered
1	clove garlic, minced
2	cups Chinese pea pods, stringed
1	cup canned sliced water chestnuts, drained
1	tablespoon sesame seeds

In a small bowl, combine vinegar, soy sauce and sugar. Set aside.

Heat oil in a wok or large skillet. Over high heat, stir-fry bell peppers and garlic for 3 minutes. Remove from wok. Add more oil to wok if necessary. Stir-fry pea pods and water chestnuts for 1 minute. Add bell peppers, sesame seeds and vinegar mixture. Toss to coat with sauce and stir-fry for 1 minute to reheat.

Greeley Street Roasted Red Potatoes

Preparation time: 20 minutes
Baking time: 30 minutes

Serves 6

2	**pounds small red potatoes, halved**
½	**teaspoon freshly ground pepper**
4	**tablespoons olive oil**
½	**teaspoon paprika**
¾	**teaspoon salt**

Preheat oven to 425°.

Toss the potatoes in oil and place them in a small roasting pan with cut side down. Sprinkle with salt, pepper and paprika.

Bake until potatoes are tender and the underside is brown and crusty, about 30 minutes. Serve at once.

Anchovy Potato Casserole

Preparation time: 30 minutes
Soaking time: 1 hour
Cooking time: 1 hour 40 minutes

Serves 6

4	**large baking potatoes**	¼	**cup butter or margarine**
1	**cup fresh onion, minced**	2½	**cups half-and-half cream**
2	**tablespoons flour**		**pimento strips or paprika (optional)**
½	**cup parsley, minced**		
1	**2-ounce can anchovies, drained and chopped**		

Wash, peel and thinly slice potatoes. Soak in ice water in refrigerator one hour. Drain and dry. Preheat oven to 450°. Combine onions, flour, parsley and anchovies in a small bowl. Arrange potatoes in 4 layers in a greased 6-cup casserole dish. Dot each layer with butter and sprinkle evenly with onion mixture. Pour cream over all. Bake 10 minutes. Reduce heat to 350° and bake 1½ hours or until potatoes are tender. Garnish with strips of pimento or dust with paprika.

Main Street Au Gratin Potatoes

Preparation time: 10 minutes
Cooking time: 1½ hours

Serves 10

1	32-ounce package of frozen hash browns, thawed
1	can each potato and celery soup
1	cup sour cream
1	small onion, grated
1¼	cups sharp cheddar cheese, grated
	salt and pepper to taste
	paprika

Preheat oven to 325°.

Mix together hash browns, soup, sour cream, onion and 1 cup of the cheese in a large bowl. Place mixture in a 9" x 13" baking dish. Top with remaining cheese and dust with paprika. Bake 1½ hours. Add milk if potatoes dry out. Cover with aluminum foil when potatoes turn brown.

Scalloped Potatoes Supreme

Preparation time: 30 minutes
Cooking time: 40 minutes

Serves 4

4	medium baking potatoes	2	tablespoons parsley, chopped
3	tablespoons butter or margarine	½	cup cheddar cheese, grated
½	teaspoon salt	½	cup half-and-half cream
⅛	teaspoon pepper		

Preheat oven to 325°.

Peel potatoes and cut into thin strips. Line a baking dish with aluminum foil. Lightly butter the foil. Place potatoes on the foil, dot with butter and sprinkle with salt, pepper, parsley and cheese. Pour cream over potatoes. Seal potatoes in foil but do not press down. Bake 40 minutes. Garnish with parsley.

Spinach Soufflé à la Florentine

Preparation time: 45 minutes

Cooking time: 1 hour

Serves 6

2	tablespoons butter or margarine
2	tablespoons flour
1	cup milk
	salt and pepper to taste
1	cup spinach, finely chopped
1	cup Swiss cheese, grated
1	teaspoon onion, finely chopped
4	egg yolks
6	egg whites, room temperature
dash	cream of tartar

Preheat oven to 350°.

Melt butter in a small skillet. Add flour and whisk for 3 minutes or until smooth. Gradually add milk, stirring constantly until smooth and thick. Add salt and pepper to taste. Then add spinach, cheese and onion. Cool. Beat egg yolks until fluffy. Add to spinach mixture. Beat egg whites with cream of tartar until peaks form. Carefully fold into spinach mixture.

Bake in ungreased 2-quart casserole in a pan of water for 1 hour or until a knife inserted in the center comes out clean.

Of special interest for the guests of the Cà d'Zan, winter home of John and Mable Ringling, were the many embellished and painted ceilings. Mounted on the ballroom ceiling, 23 canvases depict the **Dancers of the Nations.** *They were painted by Willy Pogany, set designer for Ziegfeld and the Metropolitan Opera. On the third floor, Pogany's game room ceiling takes on a festive air, depicting the Ringlings in Venetian dress, surrounded by their five pet dogs and pet birds. In the dining room, an American artist, Robert Webb, painted ceiling designs inspired by Mable's unset cameos.*

Herbed Stuffed Zucchini

Preparation time: 20 minutes
Cooking time: 30 minutes

Serves 4

4	medium zucchini
¼	pound mushrooms, chopped
¼	cup shallots, chopped
3	tablespoons butter or margarine
¼	teaspoon salt
2	tablespoons flour
1	teaspoon dried basil
¼	teaspoon freshly ground pepper
3	tablespoons sour cream
1	cup shredded Gruyère cheese

Preheat oven to 350°.

Cook whole zucchini in boiling salted water for 5 minutes. Drain. Cut off ends and slice lengthwise. Scoop out pulp, leaving ¼" shell.

Sauté mushrooms and shallots in butter for 5 minutes. Add salt and continue cooking until all the moisture evaporates. Stir in flour, basil and pepper. Cook for 2 minutes. Cool slightly and stir in sour cream and cheese. Spoon into zucchini boats. Bake 15 minutes or until hot and bubbly. If desired, sprinkle with additional cheese and broil until nicely browned.

These can be prepared a little ahead of time, and baked just before serving, allowing more time to heat through.

 Cà d'Zan is among the last of the palatial monuments to wealth and power built by rich Americans in the early 20th century. Completed in 1926, this unique structure drew decorative elements from Italian and French Renaissance, baroque, and Venetian gothic architecture. While patterned after the elegance of 17th-century Italy, the mansion projected an unmistakable aura of the ostentatious 1920s.

Phillippi Creek Italian Zucchini

Preparation time: 30 minutes   Serves 4
Cooking time: 12 minutes

1	onion, sliced thin
2	tablespoons salad oil
¼	cup water
1	pound zucchini, sliced
½	teaspoon salt
	pinch of oregano
	Italian parsley, chopped
	grated Parmesan cheese

Sauté onion in oil. Add water, zucchini, salt and oregano. Simmer 5 minutes or until tender, then raise heat to evaporate excess liquid.

Garnish with parsley and Parmesan cheese before serving.

Zucchini & Tomato Sauté

Preparation time: 20 minutes   Serves 4
Cooking time: 15 minutes

3	medium zucchini, cut into ½" slices
4 - 6	Roma tomatoes, sliced crosswise
½	small white onion, sliced
2	tablespoons butter or margarine
	salt and freshly ground pepper to taste
	sliced mushrooms (optional)

Melt butter in a skillet over medium high heat. Add onion and sauté until clear. Add squash and tomatoes, stir together and reduce heat. Cover and cook until squash is tender but not mushy.

Add salt and pepper and sliced mushrooms if desired.

Palazzo Eggplant Parmesan

Preparation time: 30 minutes
Cooking time: 30 minutes

Serves 6

½	cup flour, sifted
1½	teaspoons salt
⅜	teaspoon pepper
2	medium eggplants, peeled and cut into ½" slices
½	cup cooking oil
½	cup each onion and green pepper, chopped
1	clove garlic, chopped (optional)
2	tablespoons parsley, chopped
2	8-ounce cans tomato sauce
8	ounces sliced mozzarella cheese
¼	cup grated Parmesan cheese
	buttered bread crumbs (optional)

Preheat oven to 350°.

Combine flour, 1 teaspoon salt and ¼ teaspoon pepper. Dip eggplant in mixture and brown on both sides in oil. Drain on absorbent paper.

Sauté onion, green pepper and garlic (optional) for 5 minutes. Add parsley, tomato sauce and remaining salt and pepper. Cook 5 more minutes.

Spoon half the sauce into a 2-quart casserole dish and layer with eggplant, mozzarella cheese and remaining sauce. Sprinkle with Parmesan cheese. Cover with buttered bread crumbs, if desired. Bake 30 minutes.

One of the rare and beautiful items that John and Mable Ringling brought to Sarasota from Italy was Mable's Venetian gondola. Moored at their dock in front of the Cà d'Zan on Sarasota Bay, it sat alongside the 125-foot Ringling yacht, Zalophus.

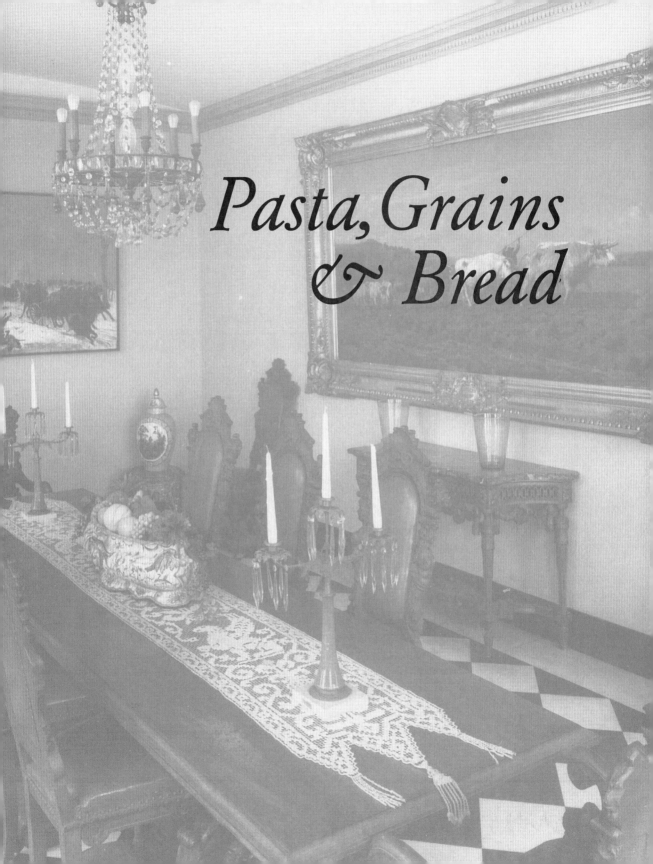

Pasta, Grains & Bread

Spanish Point Shrimp Linguine

Preparation time: 20 minutes
Cooking time: 10 minutes

Serves 4 - 6

½	**pound medium fresh shrimp, uncooked**
½	**cup butter or margarine**
1	**large green pepper, diced**
1	**bunch green onions, chopped**
1	**small can sliced ripe olives**
1	**large ripe peeled tomato, diced**
1	**pound linguine, cooked**

Boil shrimp in water until pink (3 - 5 minutes). Drain, peel and set aside. Sauté green pepper and green onion in butter until limp. Add olives, tomato and shrimp. Heat until shrimp are hot.

Pour over cooked, drained pasta and mix well. Sprinkle with freshly grated Parmesan cheese.

Fettuccine Ringling

Preparation time: 10 minutes
Cooking time: 15 minutes

Serves 4 - 6

12	**ounces fettucine noodles**
¾	**cup butter or margarine**
1	**cup whipping cream**
¼	**teaspoon white pepper**
1¼	**cups grated Parmesan cheese**
2	**teaspoons fresh parsley, chopped**
¼	**teaspoon nutmeg**

Cook fettucine according to package directions. Drain and keep warm.

Over medium heat, melt butter or margarine in a saucepan. Add whipping cream, white pepper, Parmesan cheese, parsley and nutmeg. Stir until well blended. If sauce separates, then add a little more cream. Pour over fettucine. Mix and serve immediately.

Italian Spaghetti Sauce

Preparation time: 30 minutes
Cooking time: 7 - 9 hours

Makes 10 cups

⅓	cup olive oil
4	medium onions, finely chopped
4	medium green peppers, finely chopped
1	clove garlic, minced
4	cans tomato soup, undiluted
1	6-ounce can tomato paste
1	15-ounce can tomato sauce
1	cup water
1	tablespoon Worcestershire sauce
	salt to taste
	few drops Tabasco Sauce
2	pounds ground beef or ground turkey

Heat oil in heavy kettle or Dutch oven and add onions, pepper and garlic. Stir occasionally and cook 10 - 15 minutes or until limp. Add soup, tomato paste, tomato sauce, water and seasonings. Stir well. Cover and let simmer 6 - 8 hours, stirring occasionally. The sauce will become smooth. This can be simmered in a crock pot instead of the Dutch oven.

In the meantime, brown the meat and drain off fat. Add to the sauce and simmer 1 hour. Add mushrooms, if desired.

Pour over spaghetti and sprinkle with freshly grated Parmesan cheese. Great served with Italian bread, green salad and red wine. Serve fruit and cheeses for dessert.

—•••••—

 John and Mable Ringling entertained almost constantly during their Sarasota winters in the Cà d'Zan. Their guests included leaders in the hotel and rail industries, and political and entertainment figures of the day, including Governor Alfred E. Smith and Mayor Jimmy Walker of New York, Florenz Ziegfeld, Thomas Edison, Will Rogers, and New York Giants Manager, John J. McGraw.

—•••••—

Spaghetti with Pesto Genovese

Preparation time: 20 minutes

Cooking time: 10 minutes

Serves 6

3	cups fresh basil	4	tablespoons butter
1	clove garlic, peeled	½	cup Parmesan cheese
¼	cup Italian olive oil		salt to taste
¾	cup pine nuts	2	pounds spaghetti

Wash and dry basil. Remove stems. Place in a food processor or blender with garlic, olive oil, pine nuts, butter and cheese. Process until blended.

Cook spaghetti *al dente* according to package directions. Drain and toss at once with the sauce. Add salt, if desired. Serve with additional Parmesan cheese.

Palms Elysian Pesto Sauce

Preparation time: 10 minutes

Makes 2 cups

3	cups washed fresh basil	½	teaspoon salt
4	cloves garlic, peeled	1	cup Parmesan cheese, freshly grated
1	cup pine nuts or walnuts		few shakes of pepper
1	cup good grade olive oil		

Combine basil, garlic and nuts. Put in processor and grind until fine. Add oil slowly. Then by hand, blend in salt, cheese and pepper.

Pesto is delicious tossed not only with spaghetti but with any ribbon pasta like fettuccine or tagliatelle. It is also wonderful stirred into vegetable soup or tossed through fresh steamed vegetables. It can be added to mayonnaise and used for an interesting dressing on pasta salad or potato salad. It is a wonderful, fresh-tasting sauce which originated in Genoa, Italy.

Pesto freezes well. It is best frozen in small quantities.

Hearty Lasagna

Preparation time: 30 minutes
Cooking time: 1¼ hours

Serves 10

2	pounds lean ground beef or ground turkey
1	clove garlic, minced
1	tablespoon dried parsley or 3 tablespoons fresh parsley
1	teaspoon dried basil or 3 teaspoons fresh basil
1	teaspoon dried oregano or 3 teaspoons fresh oregano
1½	teaspoons salt
2	cups tomatoes, chopped (fresh or canned)
2	6-ounce cans tomato paste
1	10-ounce package lasagna noodles
24	ounces large curd cottage cheese or ricotta cheese
2	large eggs, beaten
2	teaspoons salt
½	teaspoon pepper
2	tablespoons dried parsley or 6 tablespoons fresh parsley
½	cup Parmesan cheese
16	ounces mozzarella cheese

Preheat oven to 350°.

Brown meat lightly. Add next 7 ingredients. Simmer uncovered about 45 minutes or until thick, stirring occasionally.

Meanwhile, cook lasagna noodles according to package directions. Rinse in cold water and drain.

Combine cottage or ricotta cheese with the next 5 ingredients.

Lightly grease a 13" x 9" x 2" pan. Place ½ the noodles in the pan. Spread ½ the cheese mixture over noodles then ½ the mozzarella cheese. Layer ½ the meat sauce over cheeses. Repeat this layering once. Bake 30 minutes or until bubbly. Let stand for 10 minutes before serving.

This dish freezes well.

Baked Noodles Parmesan

Preparation time: 20 minutes
Cooking time: 30 minutes

Serves 6

1	8-ounce package noodles		1	teaspoon Worcestershire sauce
1	clove garlic, minced		½	bunch green onions, finely chopped
½	pint sour cream		½	cup Parmesan cheese, grated
¼	teaspoon Tabasco Sauce		½	pound ground beef or turkey, if desired
1½	cups cottage cheese			

Preheat oven to 350°.

Cook noodles according to package directions. Drain. In a buttered casserole dish, combine all ingredients except Parmesan cheese. Sprinkle Parmesan cheese on top. Bake 30 minutes or until bubbly. If desired, ½ pound ground beef or turkey, browned in butter or margarine, can be added to the dish before baking.

Macaroni Loaf with Mushroom Sauce

Preparation time: 15 minutes
Cooking time: 1 hour

Serves 8

1	cup macaroni			salt, to taste
1	cup bread pieces		¾	cup cheddar cheese, grated
1	cup light cream		2	ounces pimento (optional)
½	cup melted butter		1	tablespoon parsley (optional)
3	large eggs, beaten			

Preheat oven to 350°.

Cook macaroni according to package directions and drain. Combine all ingredients and put in greased 5" x 9" loaf pan. Place loaf pan in pan of water inside oven. Bake 1 hour or until knife comes out clean inserted in center. Let set for 5 minutes.

Serve with mushroom sauce. Use a medium white sauce with 8 ounces of fresh sautéed mushrooms.

Manicotti Capri

Preparation time: 30 minutes
Cooking time: 30 minutes

Serves 4

1	pound lean ground beef or ground turkey
¼	cup chopped onion
1	clove garlic, minced
1	can spinach, drained and chopped
½	cup cottage cheese or ricotta cheese
2	large eggs, slightly beaten
	salt and pepper, to taste
16	ounces spaghetti sauce (homemade or in the jar)
½	cup Parmesan cheese, grated
1	cup mozzarella cheese, shredded
12	cooked manicotti shells
3	ounces of canned or fresh mushrooms (optional)

Preheat oven to 350°.

Brown meat. Add onion and garlic, sauté about 4 minutes or until onion is tender. Drain off all fat. Remove from heat and add spinach, cottage or ricotta cheese, eggs, salt and pepper. Stir until well mixed.

Fill each manicotti shell with ¼ cup meat mixture. Place filled shells in pan and cover with spaghetti sauce. May add mushrooms to the sauce, if desired. Sprinkle with Parmesan and mozzarella cheeses. Bake 30 minutes in lightly greased 9" x 13" pan.

•••••

"The kitchen in this house is never closed," John Ringling would inform his guests. Indeed, the hearty fare of the Ringlings' German cook for 25 years, Sophie Collins, was popular among John's business guests and other visitors. Among Sophie's specialties were John's personal choice, sautéed kidneys on toast, and Mable's favorite, sweetbreads. A treasured friend, she and John conversed in German, often including John's African parrot, Jacob, who spoke German, as well.

•••••

135

Tabbouleh

Preparation time: 10 minutes
Marinating time: 45 minutes

Serves 4 - 6

2	cups coarse cracked wheat
1	teaspoon salt
½	cup each fresh parsley and mint, minced
½	cup green onion, chopped
2	tomatoes, peeled, seeded and chopped
¾	cup lemon juice
1	cup olive oil or half olive and sesame or vegetable oil salt and pepper to taste

Place cracked wheat and salt in a large earthenware casserole with a lid. Pour enough boiling water to cover and put lid on casserole. Let soak for 45 minutes. Drain excess water and add all other ingredients. Marinate for 45 minutes. This is especially good served with lamb or other grilled meat.

Hillsborough Browned Rice

Preparation time: 15 minutes
Cooking time: 1½ - 2 hours

Serves 6 - 8

1	cup long grain rice	1	can sliced mushrooms
¼	pound butter or light margarine		garlic salt to taste
1	can beef consommé		

Preheat oven to 300°.

Over medium heat, brown rice in butter. Add enough water to consommé to make 3 cups of liquid. Add to browned rice. Add mushrooms and garlic salt. Put in 9" x 13" baking pan or casserole. Cover tightly and bake 1½ - 2 hours or until all liquid has been absorbed. Stir once or twice during baking.

Great served with chicken, salad and French bread.

Still Life with Parrots
Jan Davidsz. de Heem, late 1640s, oil on canvas.

The dining room at Cà d'Zan set for Christmas dinner.

The Courtyard of the Ringling Museum is surrounded by 91 antique columns
with architectural doorways, loggias and terraces. Numerous bronze and
concrete sculptures, fountains and a reflecting pool can be found there.

Still Life with Oranges
Albert F. King, c. 1885, oil on canvas.

Angel Wings Apricot Bread

Preparation time: 20 minutes

Baking time: 45 - 60 minutes

Makes 2 loaves

1	**cup dried apricots, coarsely chopped**
½	**cup hot water**
1	**cup sugar**
1	**cup brown sugar**
3	**cups flour**
½	**teaspoon baking soda**
2	**teaspoons baking powder**
½	**teaspoons salt**
3	**large eggs, beaten**
1	**cup sour cream**
1	**cup pecans, chopped**

Preheat oven to 350°.

Soak apricots in hot water for 5 minutes.

Sift dry ingredients into large mixing bowl. Add eggs and mix until blended. Stir in sour cream and pecans. Add apricots with the hot water.

Pour into 2 greased 5" x 9" loaf pans. Bake 45 - 60 minutes. Begin checking with a toothpick for doneness at 45 minutes.

—··•·•··—

The sun room in John and Mable Ringling's Cà d'Zan, today occupied by the museum shop, was enjoyed year round. Its green marble floors and painted ceiling with an antique gilded lantern gracefully maintained the estate's grand Italian splendor. Even so, this remained the mansion's only casually appointed room. Furnished in wicker and rattan, it made for gracious, comfortable afternoons by the swimming pool with neighbors and friends.

—··•·•··—

Southern Cornbread

Preparation time: 15 minutes
Baking time: 20 minutes

Makes 1 loaf or 6 muffins

½	cup corn meal	1	tablespoon sugar
½	cup flour	1	large egg, beaten
2	teaspoons baking powder	¾	cup milk
½	teaspoon salt	2	tablespoons melted shortening

Preheat oven to 375°.

Mix dry ingredients together. Add egg and mix until well blended. Add milk and shortening. Grease 5" x 9" loaf pan or standard sized muffin pan. Pour in batter. If using muffin pan fill only ⅔ full. Bake 20 minutes or until toothpick inserted in the center comes out clean.

Salsa, green chili peppers or jalapeño peppers may be added for variety.

Autumn Pumpkin Bread

Preparation time: 20 minutes
Baking time: 1½ hours

Makes 4 loaves of 16 slices each

1	cup butter or margarine	3½	cups flour
3	cups sugar	1½	teaspoons salt
4	large eggs	1	teaspoon nutmeg
⅔	cup water	2	teaspoons baking soda
2	cups pumpkin	1	teaspoon cinnamon

Cream butter and sugar together with an electric mixer until light and fluffy. Add eggs and beat. Blend in pumpkin and water. Add dry ingredients and mix until well blended.

Grease 4 1-pound coffee cans. Pour batter into each coffee can until half full. Bake 1½ hours.

Chopped walnuts or raisins can be added for variety.

Bird Key Banana Bread

Preparation time: 20 minutes   Makes 1 loaf
Baking time: 1¼ hours

½	cup shortening	½	teaspoon salt
1	teaspoon vanilla extract	1	teaspoon baking soda
1⅓	cups light brown sugar	¼	cup buttermilk
2	large eggs, beaten	1	cup bananas, mashed
2	cups sifted flour	½	cup pecans, chopped

Preheat oven to 350°.

Cream together shortening, vanilla and sugar with electric mixer until light and fluffy. Add eggs and mix well. Add dry ingredients slowly at low speed. Stir in buttermilk, bananas and nuts. Grease 5" x 9" loaf pan. Pour in batter and bake for 1¼ hours or until toothpick comes out clean.

Daytona Date Nut Bread

Preparation time: 20 minutes   Makes 1 loaf
Baking time: 1 hour

1	cup dates, chopped	½	teaspoon salt
1	cup boiling water	1	large egg
1	teaspoon baking soda	1½	cups flour
⅔	cup light brown sugar	½	cup nuts, chopped
1	tablespoon butter		

Preheat oven to 300°.

In small bowl, combine dates, water and baking soda.

In large bowl, cream sugar and butter with an electric mixer until light and fluffy. Add salt and egg, mix well. Add flour and blend. Add date mixture and nuts. Grease a 5" x 9" loaf pan. Pour in batter and bake 1 hour or until toothpick inserted in center comes out clean.

Burns Court Rhubarb Bread

Preparation time: 20 minutes
Baking time: 1 hour 20 minutes

Makes 2 loaves

Bread
1	cup light brown sugar
½	cup granulated sugar
⅔	cup vegetable oil
1	large egg
1	cup buttermilk
1	teaspoon each salt and baking soda
2½	cups flour
1	teaspoon vanilla extract
1½	cups rhubarb, finely chopped
½	cup nuts, chopped

Topping
½	cup granulated sugar
1	tablespoon butter or margarine

Preheat oven to 325°.

Stir together brown sugar with ½ cup granulated sugar. Add oil and blend well. Add egg and beat.
Add buttermilk and blend well. Stir in salt, baking soda and flour. Add vanilla, rhubarb and nuts.
Blend well. Grease 2 5" x 9" loaf pans. Pour in batter. For topping, blend butter or margarine into
½ cup sugar with pastry cutter or fork. Sprinkle topping over loaves. Bake 1 hour 20 minutes.

———— •• ● •• ————

*The Cà d'Zan, John Ringling's palatial, ornate Sarasota residence, was a symbol
of his dreams and accomplishments. The walls of the great mansion were finished
in a sunset-pink stucco and the roof in Spanish tiles. A central hall rising two and
a half stories is surrounded by 30 rooms. The mansion featured a huge marble
terrace, a yacht channel and landing pier, tennis courts, and a long salt water pool.*

———— •• ● •• ————

Southern Puffy Spoon Bread

Preparation time: 15 minutes
Baking time: 30 minutes

Serves 6

3	large eggs, separated	1	teaspoon baking soda
2	cups buttermilk	½	teaspoon salt
½	cup white corn meal	2	tablespoons butter, melted
1	teaspoon baking powder		

Preheat oven to 375°.

Grease the sides and bottom of a 1½-quart baking dish that is at least 2½" deep. Put dish in the oven while spoon bread is being prepared. Beat egg yolks well and stir in buttermilk. Sift dry ingredients and add them to egg yolk mixture, stirring well. Add melted butter. In a separate bowl, beat egg whites until stiff. Add the egg whites to mixture, folding lightly. Spoon batter into hot baking dish and bake for 30 minutes, or until golden brown.

Zalophus Zucchini Nut Bread

Preparation time: 20 minutes
Baking time: 50 minutes

Makes 2 large or 3 small loaves

4	large eggs	1½	teaspoons salt
2	cups sugar	1	teaspoon cinnamon
1	cup vegetable oil	¾	teaspoon baking powder
1	teaspoon vanilla extract	2	cups zucchini, unpeeled and grated
3½	cups flour	1	cup nuts, chopped
1½	teaspoons baking soda		

Preheat oven to 350°.

Beat eggs and add sugar, oil and vanilla, mixing well. Add dry ingredients slowly, mixing well. Make sure zucchini is drained of water, pressing it in a colander, if necessary. Add zucchini and nuts to mixture, stirring well. Bake on low rack in oven for 50 minutes or until toothpick inserted in center comes out clean.

Panhandle Baking Powder Biscuits

Preparation time: 15 minutes
Baking time: 12 - 15 minutes

Makes 8

1	cup flour
2½	teaspoons baking powder
2	tablespoons shortening
½	teaspoon salt
¼	cup plus 2 tablespoons whole milk

Preheat oven to 425°.

Mix flour, baking powder and salt together in a large bowl. Cut in shortening with a fork or pastry blender. Add milk and blend. Do not overwork dough. Roll out dough on floured surface until ¾" thick. Cut with 2" - 2½" biscuit cutter. Bake on greased cookie sheet for 12 - 15 minutes.

These are light and delicious served with jam and honey. They also go well with fried chicken.

High Rise Popovers

Preparation time: 15 minutes
Baking time: 30 minutes

Makes 6

2	large eggs
1	cup milk
1	cup flour, sifted
½	teaspoon salt
1	tablespoon butter, melted

Break eggs into bowl. Add milk, flour, salt and melted butter. Stir all ingredients together with a spoon. The batter should be slightly lumpy. Fill 6 well-greased custard cups ⅔ full.

Put in cold oven and set temperature to 450°. Bake 30 minutes. Do not open oven door during baking. Remove popovers from the oven, prick sides to allow steam to escape. Serve immediately.

Swedish Rye Bread

Preparation time: 2 hours
Baking time: 50 minutes

Makes 4 loaves

1	**cup dark brown sugar**
½	**cup dark molasses**
2	**tablespoons shortening**
1	**tablespoon salt**
	warm water
2	**packages dry yeast**
½	**cup warm water**
4	**cups medium rye flour**
7 - 8	**cups white flour, sifted**

Preheat oven to 350°.

Combine brown sugar, molasses and shortening in medium pot. Bring to a boil until sugar is almost dissolved. Add salt. Add enough warm water so that the entire mixture measures 5 cups of liquid, and transfer to a large mixing bowl.

Dissolve yeast in warm water. Add to mixture. Beat in rye flour and 7 cups white flour and knead. If dough is still sticky gradually add more white flour so it can be easily kneaded.

Let rise in warm place until double in bulk, approximately 4 hours.

Make into 4 loaves and let rise two hours. Bake 50 minutes (check bread at 40 minutes, if loaves are getting too brown lower oven temperature for the last 10 minutes).

Above Mable Ringling's dining table in the Cà d'Zan, a silver chandelier of Moorish design gleamed in the soft light. Silver wall sconces added to the air of opulence, as did Mable's gold and ivory Lenox dinner service which graced the table beside monogrammed, crystal stemware.

Dinner Rolls

Preparation time: 3 hours
Baking time: 15 - 20 minutes

Makes 5 dozen

1	cup boiling water
2	heaping tablespoons shortening (or half butter)
½	cup sugar
2	teaspoons salt
1	cup cold water

2	packages dry yeast
4	tablespoons warm water
2	large eggs, beaten
8	cups flour
	melted butter

Preheat oven to 375°.

In a large bowl, combine the boiling water, shortening, sugar and salt. Stir until dissolved. Add the cold water to make the mixture lukewarm. Then add the yeast which has been softened in 4 tablespoons of warm water. Add eggs and gradually stir in flour to form soft dough.

Knead dough on lightly floured board for 6 - 8 minutes adding flour if necessary so dough can be easily handled. Cover with a towel and let rise in a warm place until double in bulk, about 2 hours.

Turn out on a lightly floured surface and roll ½" thick. Cut with 2½" biscuit cutter. Brush with melted butter, crease in half and fold over. Allow to double in size.

Bake 15 - 20 minutes, or until very light brown on top. Remove from baking pan and cool on baking racks.

—•●•—

Mable Ringling loved the Cà d'Zan's formal dining room with its English walnut paneling. In contrast to Mable's large afternoon musicales and bridge parties, her dinner parties were more intimate in size and character. Gentlemen invited to the Ringling table were customarily given a card naming the woman each was to escort in to dinner. On such formal occasions, a servant stood behind every two guests, ready to oblige any requests. In spite of Prohibition, guests always found their glasses filled with the finest wines and liqueurs.

—•●•—

Big Pass Blueberry Muffins

Preparation time: 20 minutes
Baking time: 30 minutes

Makes 8 muffins

2	cups flour	1	large egg, lightly beaten
4	teaspoons baking powder	¾	cup milk
1	teaspoon salt	3	tablespoons butter, melted
½	cup sugar	1	cup blueberries, dredged in flour

Preheat oven to 375°.

Sift together flour, baking powder and salt. Add sugar, egg, milk and butter and stir just until blended. Fold in blueberries carefully. Grease muffins tins and fill them ⅔ full. Bake 25 - 30 minutes or until done.

For half a recipe, use ⅓ cup of milk.

Clown Alley Pancakes

Preparation time: 10 minutes
Cooking time: 10 minutes

Makes 3 servings

2	large eggs, beaten	1	cup buttermilk
2	heaping tablespoons sugar	1	teaspoon baking soda
	pinch of salt	¼	teaspoon baking powder
1¼	cups flour		

Preheat griddle or electric frying pan to 425°.

Mix eggs, sugar, salt and flour together by hand or with electric mixer. In a separate bowl, mix buttermilk with baking soda. Add to batter along with baking powder. Drop spoonfuls onto hot griddle and cook until golden brown on each side.

These are light and fluffy and delicious with wild blueberries sprinkled in the batter.

Beachside Bran Muffins

Preparation time: 20 minutes
Baking time: 20 - 25 minutes

Makes 30 large muffins

3	cups bran cereal
1	cup boiling water
1½	cups sugar
½	cup butter or margarine
2	large eggs
2½	teaspoons baking soda
½	tablespoon salt
2½	cups flour
2	cups buttermilk

Preheat oven to 375°.

Soak 2 cups of cereal in boiling water for 1 hour.

In separate bowl, cream the sugar and butter or margarine with an electric mixer until light and fluffy. Add eggs and mix well. Sift baking soda, salt and flour together and add slowly to creamed mixture, alternating with buttermilk. Add the remaining 1 cup of dry cereal to soaked cereal mixture. Add this to batter. Grease muffin tins and fill ½ - ¾ with the batter. Bake 20 - 25 minutes or until done.

This batter can be kept in the refrigerator for up to 4 weeks.

---

 *The gracious and convivial atmosphere of the dining room in John and Mable Ringling's Cà d'Zan was created in part by an intricate overmantle wreath festooned with garlic buds, a symbol of hospitality. The wreath came from the della Robbia studios in Florence. Over the buffet, Giovanni Granieri's **A Crowded Market Place** (1756) added to the room's charm, while at the dining room's entrance hung the **Portrait of Mariana of Austria**, then attributed to Velázquez.*

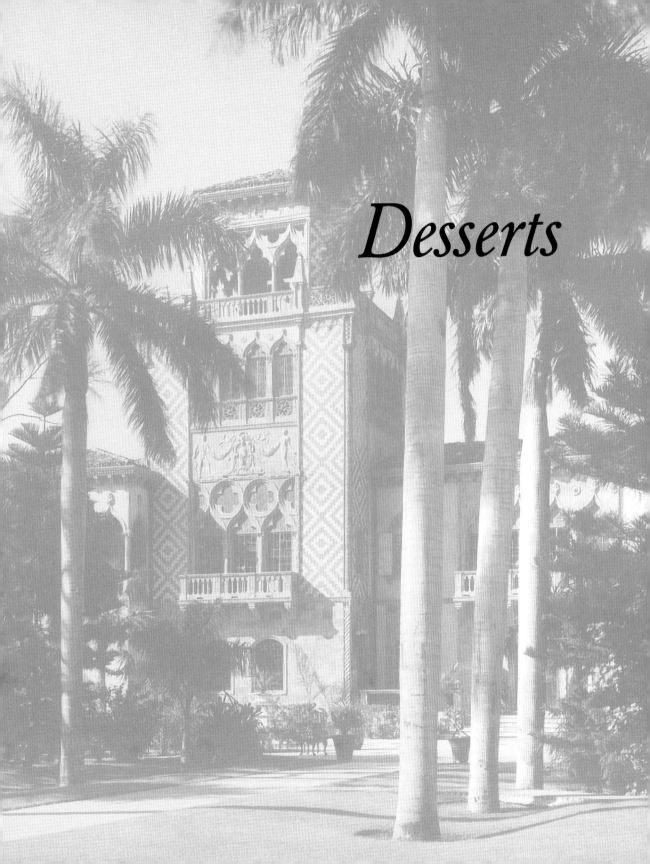

Desserts

Sunset Lime Soufflé

Preparation time: 30 minutes
Chilling time: 6 hours

Serves 8 - 10

8	large eggs, separated
1½	cups extra fine sugar
½	cup lime juice
½	teaspoon salt
2	envelopes gelatin, softened in ⅓ cups water
1	tablespoon grated lime zest
2	cups heavy cream
	kiwi slices, strawberries or toasted coconut flakes

In top of double boiler mix egg yolks with ½ cup sugar, lime juice and salt. Cook over simmering water, stirring until slightly thickened.

Remove from heat and stir in gelatin and lime zest until completely dissolved. Set aside and cool.

Beat egg whites until they hold soft peaks and gradually beat in 1 cup sugar. Set aside.

Beat cream until it holds its shape. Gently fold whites and cream into lime mixture. Spoon into 2-quart soufflé dish and chill for at least 6 hours.

Decorate with thin slices of kiwi, strawberries, or toasted coconut flakes.

—————————•••••—————————

 The historic 19th-century Asolo theater, which once entertained royalty and aristocrats in the ancient Italian town of Asolo, today stands reconstructed adjoining the Art Museum. From its purchase in 1950 until the early '80s, this charming baroque-style playhouse added grace to each performance with its elaborate decoration, tiered seating, and 10 portrait medallions of famous Italian poets and playwrights.

—————————•••••—————————

Frozen Grand Marnier Soufflé

Preparation time: 20 minutes
Freezing time: 8 hours or overnight

Serves 10

Soufflé
½   gallon vanilla ice cream
8   macaroons, dried and crumbled
8   tablespoons Grand Marnier
1   cup heavy cream, whipped

Strawberry Sauce
2   pints strawberries
2   tablespoons sugar
6   tablespoons Grand Marnier

Soften ice cream in a large bowl. Add macaroons and Grand Marnier. Fold in whipped cream. Pour into 3-quart mold and freeze overnight. Unmold on serving dish and serve with strawberry sauce. To make strawberry sauce, wash and hull berries. Add sugar and heat until soft but not mushy. Add liqueur and serve warm.

Palm Avenue Meringues

Preparation time: 15 minutes
Cooking time: 45 - 60 minutes

Makes 18

7   large egg whites
2¼   cups sugar
¼   teaspoon salt
1   teaspoon vanilla extract

Preheat oven to 225°.

Beat egg whites until stiff. Add 1½ cups sifted sugar and salt very gradually and beat until very stiff. Add vanilla and fold in remaining sugar. Spoon 18 mounds of mixture on greased and floured cookie sheet. Bake 45 - 60 minutes. Cool. Meringues freeze well. Fill with ice cream and fruit or custard.

Frosted Peaches with Ladyfingers

Preparation time: 30 minutes
Freezing time: 8 hours

Serves 8

2	10-ounce packages frozen sliced peaches	1	teaspoon sugar
12	ladyfingers, split	½	teaspoon vanilla or almond extract
	peach brandy	½	cup almonds, toasted and finely chopped
½	pint whipping cream		

Partially thaw peaches. Cover bottom and sides of 8" square pan with split ladyfingers. Moisten lightly with brandy and cover with peach slices. Whip cream, add sugar and extract. Top ladyfingers and peaches with the cream mixture. Sprinkle with toasted almonds. Cover with wax paper and freeze 8 hours.

Remove from freezer 20 minutes before serving. Cut in narrow slices to serve.

Pinellas Peach Melba

Preparation time: 30 minutes
Standing time: 2 - 3 hours

Serves 8

Peaches
1½	cups sugar
2	cups water
4	peaches, peeled and halved

Raspberry Sauce
1	pint raspberries
½	cup sugar
1	quart vanilla ice cream

In a pan over medium heat combine sugar and water and bring to a boil until sugar is dissolved. Add peaches and simmer until tender. Set aside. For sauce, sprinkle berries with sugar and let stand 2 - 3 hours. Puree in blender and put through sieve. To serve, place a peach half over a scoop of vanilla ice cream and cover with raspberry sauce.

Mother's Apple Crisp

Preparation time: 20 minutes

Cooking time: 30 minutes

Serves 9

Apple Crisp
6	tart apples, peeled and sliced
½	cup sugar
½	cup water
1	cup brown sugar
1	cup flour
1	teaspoon baking powder
½	cup butter or margarine

Vanilla sauce
1	cup sugar
2 - 3	tablespoons cornstarch
⅛	teaspoon salt
2	cups boiling water
4	tablespoons butter
2	teaspoons vanilla extract
dash	nutmeg
6	tablespoons lemon juice (optional)

Preheat oven to 350°.

Cook apples in sugar and water for 10 minutes. Put in 9" square pan. Mix brown sugar, flour, baking powder and butter. Cover apples with mixture. Bake 30 minutes.

To make vanilla sauce, combine sugar, cornstarch and salt in saucepan. Add boiling water gradually, stirring constantly until clear and thick. Simmer over low heat for 5 minutes. Stir in remaining ingredients.

Optional: this becomes a delicious lemon sauce by substituting 6 tablespoons lemon juice for the vanilla extract and increasing the cornstarch to 3 tablespoons.

Serve apple crisp warm with vanilla or lemon sauce.

Summertime Rhubarb in Cream

Preparation time: 15 minutes
Chilling time: 8 hours

Serves 6 - 8

6	**cups fresh rhubarb, cubed**
2	**cups sugar**
1	**cup heavy cream, whipped**

Cook rhubarb and sugar in medium pan over medium heat. Cook until rhubarb is tender not mushy, stirring once or twice. Add more sugar if too tart.

Cool to room temperature.

Fold whipped cream into rhubarb. Place in glass bowl and chill 8 hours. It will separate into layers. Serve chilled.

Side Show Cranberry Sherbet

Preparation time: 30 minutes
Freezing time: 8 hours or overnight

Makes about 1½ quarts

1	**pound cranberries, washed (4 cups)**
2	**cups water**
2	**cups sugar**
1	**teaspoon plain gelatin**
1	**cup orange juice**
¼	**cup lemon juice**

In a medium-size pan over medium heat, cook cranberries in water about 8 - 10 minutes. Put cranberries through food mill to strain out skin, seeds and fiber. Return strained cranberries to heat. Add sugar and bring to a boil.

In a separate bowl, dissolve gelatin in fruit juices. Add to cranberries and mix well. Place mixture in 2-quart container in freezer. When partially frozen, beat well. Then refreeze until ready to serve.

Frozen Lemon Delight

Preparation time: 30 minutes   Makes 9 slices
Freezing time: 8 hours or overnight

3	**large eggs, separated**
¾	**cup sugar**
4	**tablespoons lemon juice**
1	**teaspoon lemon zest**
1	**cup heavy cream, whipped**
1	**cup vanilla wafers, crushed**

In double boiler cook egg yolks, sugar, lemon juice and zest until thick. Cool.

Add beaten egg whites and whipped cream. Cover bottom of 9" square pan with crushed wafers and add filling. Sprinkle more crushed wafers on top and freeze.

Lightning Lemon Ice

Preparation time: 20 minutes   Makes about 1 pint
Freezing time: 8 hours or overnight

½	**cup sugar**
½	**cup boiling water**
1	**cup cold water**
¼	**teaspoon grated lemon zest**
½	**cup lemon juice**

In a bowl dissolve sugar in boiling water. Add cold water, lemon zest and lemon juice. Mix well. Pour into loaf pan and freeze, about 4 hours, or until icy. Stir mixture then refreeze for 2 - 3 hours, stirring every 30 minutes. Can be frozen overnight.

Before serving, if frozen overnight, place mixture in blender and blend until fluffy.

A refreshing end to a special meal.

Helen's Chocolate Ice Box Cake

Preparation time: 30 minutes
Chilling time: 2 hours

½	**pound German sweet chocolate**
2½	**tablespoons water**
2	**tablespoons powered sugar**
dash	**salt**
4	**large eggs, separated**
1½	**dozen ladyfingers, split**
	whipped cream

Using a double boiler, melt chocolate in water with sugar and salt. Remove from heat and let cool until lukewarm. then add the 4 egg yolks one at a time beating after each addition until blended.

Beat egg whites until stiff and fold into above mixture.

Place ½ of the ladyfingers right side down on a serving plate. Fill with ½ the chocolate mixture and cover with remaining ladyfingers.

Spread remaining chocolate mixture over all. Chill until firm.

To serve, top with whipped cream.

Mable Ringling's glorious rose garden added an air of cosmopolitan elegance to the lawn surrounding their Sarasota home, the Cà d'Zan. Designed in concentric circles, 2,000 feet of curb were required to shape the gardens. In the center, a graceful English gazebo, now restored and a popular site for summer weddings, offered benches for visitors. Around the sides, white columns surrounded by a trellis for vines gave the whole a balanced, classic beauty that delighted Mable.

Macaroon & Fruit Sherbet Dessert

Preparation time: 30 minutes
Freezing time: 8 hours or overnight

Serves 12

1	**pint whipping cream**
2	**tablespoons powdered sugar, sifted**
1	**teaspoon vanilla extract**
18	**macaroons, crumbled**
3	**pints raspberry, lime and orange sherbet**
	toasted almonds

In a mixing bowl, whip cream and add sugar, vanilla and macaroons.

Spread ½ of mixture on bottom of a 9" x 13" greased cake pan. Spoon on sherbet, cover with remaining cream mixture and sprinkle with toasted almonds. Freeze.

Grand Marnier Strawberry Ice

Preparation time: 20 minutes
Soaking time: 4 hours
Freezing time: 6 - 8 hours

Makes about 1 quart

3	**pints strawberries**
2	**cups sugar**
3	**medium oranges, juiced**
3	**medium lemons, juiced**
⅓	**cup Grand Marnier**

In a medium bowl, mix berries, sugar and juices. Let soak for 4 hours.

Put mixture into blender. Add liqueur. Blend thoroughly. Pour into quart container and place in freezer.

Freeze 6 - 8 hours, beating often.

Hot Fudge Ice Cream Roll

Preparation time: 45 minutes
Baking time: 20 minutes

Serves 8

Ice Cream Roll

5	large eggs, separated
¾	cup powdered sugar
2	tablespoons cocoa
1	tablespoon flour
1½	quarts vanilla ice cream

Hot Fudge Sauce

1	tablespoon buster
1½	squares unsweetened chocolate
1	cup sugar
½	cup boiling water
2	tablespoons corn syrup
	pinch of salt
1	tablespoon vanilla extract

Preheat oven to 325°.

Lightly grease jelly-roll pan (15½" x 10½" x 1") and line bottom with wax paper.

Beat egg yolks and sugar until lemon colored. Beat egg whites until stiff and fold into yolk mixture. Sift cocoa and flour together and add to egg mixture. Bake in prepared pan 20 minutes.

Loosen sides and turn out on a hot, damp towel. Remove crusts and roll quickly.

When cool unroll and fill with ice cream. Reroll and freeze 8 hours or overnight.

To make hot fudge sauce, melt butter with chocolate. Add next 4 ingredients and cook over medium heat until thick, about 5 minutes. Add vanilla extract. Serve hot, over ice cream roll.

Bay Isles Bourbon Mint Ice Cream

Preparation time: 30 minutes
Cooking time: 20 minutes
Freezing time: follow manufacturer's instructions

Makes 1 quart

2	**cups milk**
¼	**cup bourbon**
2	**tablespoons fresh mint, chopped**
3	**large eggs**
1	**cup sugar**
½	**teaspoon salt**
1½	**cups heavy cream**
1½	**teaspoons vanilla extract**

Use this recipe with an electric ice cream maker.

Place milk, bourbon and mint in a sauce pan and bring just to a boil. Lower heat.

Meanwhile, beat eggs, sugar and salt until lemon yellow. Pour a little milk mixture into eggs first, then add the rest of the mixture slowly, stirring constantly.

Return to low heat and cook 10 minutes, stirring constantly. Strain and cool in refrigerator. Add cream and vanilla.

Pour into ice cream maker and follow manufacturer's instructions for freezing.

———•••••◦•———

 Among the more unusual of the 400 types of trees and plants found throughout the John and Mable Ringling estate and Museum grounds are the False Banyans. Seedlings for the trees were a gift to John and Mable from their friend, Thomas Edison, who lived south of Sarasota in Fort Myers. Today, these trees, with their curious roots, are enjoyed by visitors year-round.

———•••••◦•———

Caramel Sauce for Ice Cream

Preparation time: 10 minutes
Cooking time: 15 minutes

Makes 1 cup sauce

1	cup brown sugar
4	tablespoons hot water
3	tablespoons butter or margarine
1	cup cream (optional)

Put ingredients into a pan over medium heat. Bring to a boil, and immediately remove from heat. Cool and serve with pecans over ice cream.

For a richer sauce, substitute 1 cup cream for the hot water and butter. Cook in double boiler over hot water for 30 minutes.

Tallahassee Macaroon Biscuit Tortoni

Preparation time: 30 minutes
Freezing time: 4 - 6 hours

Serves 4 - 6

2	large eggs, separated
½	cup powered sugar
2	tablespoons sherry
1	teaspoon vanilla
1	cup heavy cream, whipped
⅔	cup crushed macaroons (Italian style if possible)

Beat egg yolks lightly, add sugar and beat until smooth and frothy. Stir in sherry and vanilla.

In separate bowl beat whites until stiff. Fold yolks into whites, then add whipped cream. Stir in ½ cup crushed macaroons.

Pour into individual cups and sprinkle with crumbs. Freeze.

Courtyard Crème Caramel

Preparation time: 20 minutes
Baking time: 30 minutes
Refrigeration time: 1 hour

Serves 8 - 10

Caramel
1	cup sugar
½	cup water

Custard
4	large eggs
4	large eggs, separated, yolks only
⅔	cup sugar
4	cups milk, scalded
3	teaspoons vanilla extract

Preheat oven to 350°.

To prepare caramel, heat sugar and water until sugar is dissolved. Boil until golden brown. Remove from heat.

To prepare custard, beat eggs, egg yolks and sugar, then add to scalded milk. Spoon caramel into custard cups coating the bottom and a little up the sides. Spoon in custard. Set custard cups in a pan of water, ¼" - ½" deep. Bake 30 minutes or until knife inserted in the center comes out clean. Cool. Refrigerate about 1 hour. Unmold and serve.

———··•●•··———

Without a doubt, John Ringling will always be remembered for bringing us the greatest show on earth. In 1948, two years after assuming ownership of The John and Mable Ringling Museum of Art, the State of Florida honored this great showman by establishing a circus museum. A permanent collection of circus art and artifacts is on display, including posters, photographs, costumes, and props used by famous performers and carefully restored, rare, carved circus wagons.

———··•●•··———

Semifreddo al Cioccolate Mousse

Preparation time: 45 minutes   Serves 8
Freezing time: 12 hours

> **5**   **ounces semisweet chocolate**
> **3**   **tablespoons water**
> **3**   **tablespoons sugar**
> **3**   **large egg yolks**
> **1**   **cup whipping cream**

Lightly oil 8 custard cups or ramekins. Line with plastic wrap leaving a 3" overlap.

Melt chocolate and water in double boiler over hot water. Stir constantly until melted and smooth. Add sugar and continue stirring until sugar has melted. Remove from heat. Cool.

Fold in egg yolks one at a time. Set aside.

Whip cream until soft peaks form. Fold into chocolate mixture. Fill cups with chocolate mixture close plastic wrap. Freeze 12 hours.

Remove from freezer to refrigerator 15 minutes before serving. Unwrap and unmold on a dessert plate.

Garnish with berries or whipped cream and chocolate shavings.

- - - - ··•··- - - -

 A whimsical group of folk tale characters in the Dwarf Garden are among the delightful, Italian garden sculptures throughout the 63 acres of grounds at the Ringling Museum. Charming cast-stone statues welcome visitors along the Museum drive, the approach to the rose garden and the courtyard garden.

- - - - ··•··- - - -

Chocolate-Dipped Strawberries

Preparation time: 45 minutes   Makes 30 strawberries
Refrigeration time: 1 - 2 hours

½	cup semisweet chocolate morsels
1½	tablespoons butter
1	tablespoon corn syrup
1	tablespoon dark rum
30	large strawberries, caps intact

Wash and gently dry strawberries.

In top of double boiler, over hot water, combine chocolate morsels, butter, corn syrup and rum until melted. With tongs pick up berries at stem end and dip about ⅔ of the berry into the chocolate mixture. Allow excess chocolate to drip off and place on waxed paper on cookie sheet. Refrigerate to set.

Alpine White Chocolate Truffles

Preparation time: 30 minutes   Makes 24 truffles
Chilling time: 15 minutes

8	ounces white chocolate
6	tablespoons unsalted butter, room temperature
1½	tablespoons water
1	large egg yolk
¼	cup powered sugar
¼	toasted coconut
¼	white chocolate shavings

Melt chocolate, butter and water in double boiler over hot water. Pour into bowl and add egg yolk. Continue beating until mixture is fluffy and cooled to room temperature. Chill until firm.

Remove from refrigerator and form into 1" balls. Roll in powered sugar, toasted coconut or white chocolate shavings. Chill until ready to serve.

Coffee Almond Mousse

Preparation time: 30 minutes
Freezing time: 2 - 4 hours

Serves 6 - 8

1	**large egg white**
1	**tablespoon instant coffee**
⅛	**teaspoon salt**
2	**tablespoons sugar**
1	**cup whipping cream**
¼	**cup sugar**
1	**teaspoon vanilla extract**
⅛	**teaspoon almond extract**
¼	**cup toasted almonds, finely chopped**
	few drops crème de cacao

Beat egg white until stiff, add coffee, salt and sugar. Beat until stiff and shiny.

Whip cream with extracts and remaining sugar and fold into egg mixture. Add nuts. Pour into 6 - 8 individual foil baking cup liners, filling each with ⅓ cup mousse. Freeze.

To serve, top with crème de cacao.

Suncoast Broiled Grapefruit

Preparation time: 10 minutes

Serves 2

1	**large grapefruit**
2	**tablespoons brown sugar**

Cut grapefruit in half and around each section and remove center.

Sprinkle each half with 1 tablespoon of sugar and place under broiler until sugar melts and edge of grapefruit turns a delicate brown.

Pies &
Cakes

Pastry for Pies

Preparation time: 30 minutes
Chilling time: 30 minutes
Baking time: 10 minutes

Makes 2 pie shells

2	cups unbleached sifted flour
1½	teaspoons sugar
½	teaspoon salt
½	cup cold corn oil margarine
1½	teaspoons white or cider vinegar
1	large egg white
2	tablespoons ice water

Preheat oven to 450°.

Place first 4 ingredients in large bowl. Mix well with table fork until ingredients are crumbly.

In small bowl, beat together vinegar and egg white with fork. Add this to flour mixture and stir until all ingredients are moistened. Add water, 1 tablespoon at a time, until dough forms dime-sized pieces. Divide dough into 2 portions. Wrap in wax paper and chill at least 30 minutes before rolling.

When ready to roll, lightly flour both sides of dough and roll to ⅛" thickness and larger than inverted pie pan. Put in pie pan. Prick bottom and sides before baking.

Bake about 10 minutes or until light golden brown.

—·•●•·—

 The management of the young Ringling Bros. Circus was divided among the five Ringling brothers, as each assumed a role suited to his talents. John Ringling was the route agent. The naturally frugal Otto became treasurer. Alf T. played to audiences as leader of the band, and later was head of publicity. Charles was manager of the performers and support crew who brought the circus to life. And brother Al donned high hat and tailored jacket as ringmaster and equestrian director.

—·•●•·—

French Silk Pie

Preparation time: 20 minutes   Serves 6
Chilling time: 4 - 6 hours

Crust
1   9" or 10" prepared pie crust

Filling
1   cup sweet butter
1½   cups sugar, super fine
2   teaspoons vanilla extract
½   teaspoon almond extract
3   ounces unsweetened chocolate, melted
4   large eggs
       pinch of salt

In bowl, cream butter and sugar. Add extracts and chocolate, blend. Beat eggs in one at a time. Pour into crust and chill 4 - 6 hours. Very rich and delicious!

Mississippi Mud Pie

Preparation time: 30 minutes   Serves 6
Baking time: 30 minutes

½   cup butter   1½   cups sugar
3   ounces unsweetened chocolate   1   teaspoon vanilla
3   large eggs   1   unbaked pie shell
3   tablespoons white corn syrup   vanilla ice cream

Preheat oven to 350°.

In a saucepan, combine butter and chocolate. Heat slowly, stirring until melted and blended. In bowl, beat eggs. Stir in corn syrup, sugar and vanilla. Pour into chocolate mixture. Blend well. Pour filling into pie shell. Bake 30 minutes or until filling is set. Serve warm. Top with vanilla ice cream.

Grandma's Raisin Pie

Preparation time: 10 minutes   Serves 6
Baking time: 40 minutes

2	large eggs, beaten	½	teaspoon nutmeg
1	cup sour cream	½	teaspoon cinnamon
1	cup sugar	1	teaspoon lemon juice
1	tablespoon flour	1	cup raisins, chopped
⅛	teaspoon each baking soda and salt	2	8" pie shells, top and bottom crust

Preheat oven to 450°.

Beat together eggs, sugar and sour cream. Add all other ingredients. Place filling in bottom pie shell and cover with top crust. Pierce top crust with fork. Bake at 450° 10 minutes. Lower heat to 350° and bake about 30 minutes longer.

Brandy Alexander Pie

Preparation time: 40 minutes   Serves 6
Chilling time: 8 hours or overnight

1	envelope unflavored gelatin	¼	cup cognac
¼	cup cold water	¼	cup crème de cacao
⅔	cup sugar	2	cups heavy cream
⅛	teaspoon salt	1	9" graham cracker crust
3	large eggs, separated		chocolate curls or grated chocolate

Soften gelatin in cold water in small saucepan. Add ⅓ cup sugar, salt and egg yolks. Stir to blend. Heat over simmering water in double boiler, stirring until gelatin dissolves and thickens. Remove from heat. Stir in cognac and crème de cacao.

Chill until mixture starts to mound slightly when stirred, about 30 minutes. In a bowl, with electric mixer beat egg whites until stiff. Gradually beat remaining sugar into egg whites. Fold into chilled mixture. Whip 1 cup heavy cream and fold into mixture. Turn filling into crust. Chill for 8 hours or overnight. Whip remaining cream, place on pie and garnish with chocolate curls.

Florida Key Lime Pie

Preparation time: 1 hour
Chilling time: 4 - 6 hours

Serves 6

1	cup sugar
1	tablespoon unflavored gelatin
⅛	teaspoon salt
½	cup lime juice
¼	cup water
4	large eggs, separated
	grated lime zest
1 - 2	drops green food coloring (optional)
1	cup cream, whipped
1	baked 9" pie shell

Combine gelatin, salt and ½ cup sugar in a saucepan. Beat yolks, lime juice, and water. Add to gelatin mixture.

Cook over medium heat, stirring constantly until mixture comes to a boil. Remove from heat immediately. Add grated peel and food coloring. Chill for 30 minutes. Stir occasionally to keep mixture smooth.

In bowl, beat egg whites until stiff, adding ½ cup sugar gradually. Fold chilled mixture into egg whites and add cream.

Fill pastry shell and chill 4 - 6 hours.

The Ringling brothers brought talent, enthusiasm and great determination to the ring of their tiny start-up circus. Although the two older brothers could claim some circus experience, business experience and cash reserves were another story. Lacking business knowledge, the Ringlings instead capitalized on a wealth of imagination and personality to create a vibrant, captivating show that appealed to family audiences with its good, clean fun.

Lauderdale Lemon Meringue Pie

Preparation time: 30 minutes

Baking time: 10 minutes

Chilling time: 4 - 6 hours

Serves 6

Filling
1½	cups sugar
5	tablespoons cornstarch
½	teaspoon salt
1½	cups boiling water
2	teaspoons butter or margarine
4	large eggs, separated
½	cup lemon juice
	grated lemon zest
	baked pastry shell

Meringue
4	egg whites
¼	teaspoon cream of tartar
8	teaspoons sugar

Preheat oven to 325°.

Mix sugar, cornstarch and salt in saucepan. Add boiling water and stir constantly until thick.

Add butter and 4 egg yolks slightly beaten. Cook 2 minutes over medium heat. Add lemon juice and zest. Cook until thickened. Pour into baked pastry shell.

For meringue, beat egg whites until almost stiff. Add cream of tartar and sugar and slowly beat until stiff. Spread over lemon filling.

Bake in preheated oven until lightly brown, about 10 minutes.

Chill 4 - 6 hours.

Ringling Bros., c. 1898, Poster, lithograph, Courier Company.

The Five Graces Bandwagon, built in 1878, was later acquired by Ringling Bros. and Barnum & Bailey Circus. Hand-carved and inset with gold leaf, it was pulled by a 10-horse team. It is on display in the Circus Museum of the Ringling Museum Complex.

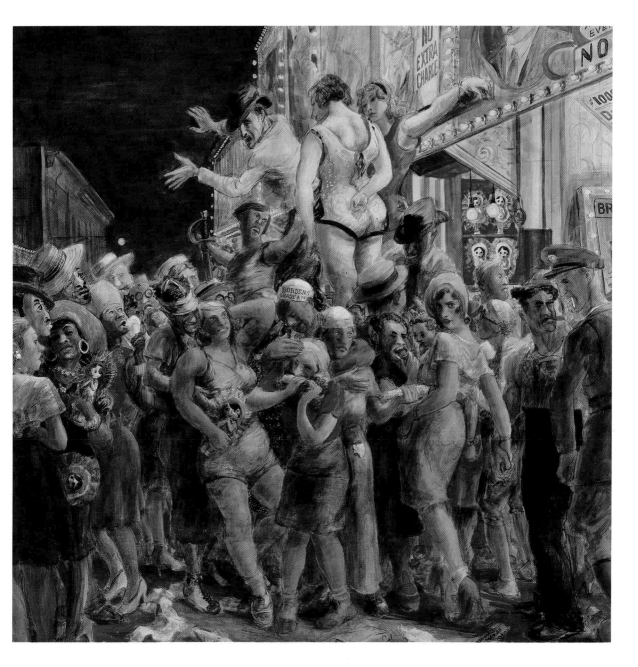

Wonderland Circus, Sideshow, Coney Island
Reginald Marsh, 1930, tempera on canvas mounted on masonite.

Salome
Robert Henri, 1909
Oil on canvas

Paradise Peach Pie

Preparation time: 15 minutes
Baking time: 30 minutes

Serves 6

½	cup butter or margarine
1	cup sugar
2	tablespoons flour
2	teaspoons vanilla
2	large eggs
1	large can sliced peaches, drained
1	9" unbaked pie shell

Preheat oven to 350°.

Mix first 5 ingredients well. Place peaches in unbaked pie shell. Pour above mixture over peaches. Bake until set, about 30 minutes.

Georgia Pecan Pie

Preparation time: 30 minutes
Baking time: 40 minutes

Serves 6

2	large eggs, beaten
1	cup brown sugar
1	cup white corn syrup
¼	teaspoon salt
2	teaspoons flour
2	tablespoons butter, melted
1	9" unbaked pie shell
1	cup pecan halves

Preheat oven to 400°.

Mix first 6 ingredients together. Pour into unbaked pie shell. Place pecan halves over top. Bake at 400° for 10 minutes, then at 350° for 30 minutes or until knife inserted in center comes out clean.

Royal Palm Rhubarb Pie

Preparation time: 30 minutes
Baking time: 40 minutes

Serves 6 - 8

Crust
½	cup butter or margarine, softened
1	tablespoon sugar
1	cup sifted flour

Filling
4	cups rhubarb, finely chopped
½	cup sugar
¼	cup flour

Topping
1	8-ounce package cream cheese, softened
⅓	cup sugar
1	large egg
½	cup sour cream
2	teaspoons sugar

Preheat oven to 425°.

To make crust, mix butter, 1 tablespoon sugar and flour together. Pat into 9" pie plate. For filling, mix rhubarb, ½ cup sugar and flour. Put into pie shell. Bake in preheated oven for 10 minutes. Remove from oven and lower oven temperature to 350°.

To make topping, blend cream cheese, ⅓ cup sugar and egg. Spread over warm pie. Mix sour cream and 2 teaspoons sugar. Spread over cream cheese layer. Bake in oven at 350° for 30 minutes.

The Ringling Bros. Circus first raised its tent flaps and captivated audiences in 1884 in the small town of Baraboo, Wisconsin. The five Ringling brothers began with 44 horses, a crew of 35 and an impressive homemade tent that seated 600.

Black Bottom Cupcakes

Preparation time: 45 minutes

Baking time: 20 minutes

Makes 24 cupcakes

Cupcakes
3	cups flour, sifted
½	cup cocoa
2	cups sugar
1	tablespoon baking soda
1	teaspoon salt
2	cups water
2	tablespoons vinegar
⅔	cup salad oil
2	teaspoons vanilla extract

Topping
1	8-ounce package cream cheese
1	large egg, beaten
1	tablespoon sugar
⅛	teaspoon salt
6	ounces semisweet chocolate morsels

Preheat oven to 350°.

To make cupcakes, sift first 5 ingredients together. Add remaining ingredients, beating well. Mixture will be stiff, continue beating.

To make topping, combine first 4 ingredients and mix by hand. Stir in chocolate morsels.

Use muffin tins and paper liners. Fill each cup ½ - ¾ full with flour mixture. Then drop one tablespoon of the cheese mixture on top of each. Bake for 20 minutes in preheated oven.

These cupcakes can be frozen successfully.

Easy Chocolate Torte

Preparation time: 30 minutes
Cooling time: 1 hour or more
Refrigeration time: 1 - 2 hours

Serves 8

1	**12-ounce pound cake**
1	**6-ounce package semisweet chocolate morsels**
½	**cup butter or margarine**
¼	**cup water**
2	**tablespoons powdered sugar**
1	**teaspoon vanilla extract**
4	**large egg yolks, slightly beaten**

Slice pound cake horizontally into six slices.

Heat chocolate, butter and water over low heat. Stir until blended. Cool slightly. Add sugar, vanilla and beaten yolks. Cool about 1 hour.

Spread mixture over each layer, rebuilding the cake. Then frost all around.

Refrigerate until firm.

To serve, slice about ½" thick.

The early Ringling Bros. Circus was one of 70 small Wisconsin circuses formed in the late 1800s. Like the others, it suffered its share of harsh weather, wagon wrecks and animal diseases. Yet, with great resolve and good judgment of audience tastes, the Ringling brothers overcame their misfortunes and fought to command first place among their competitors. For 40 years and more than 19,000 performances, one or more of the Ringling brothers personally supervised each and every performance.

Big Top Chocolate Cake

Preparation time: 30 minutes
Baking time: 50 minutes

⅔	cup butter or margarine	2	teaspoons vanilla extract
4	squares unsweetened chocolate	¼	teaspoon salt
4	large eggs	1	cup sifted cake flour
2	cups sugar	1	teaspoon baking powder

Preheat oven to 350°.

Melt chocolate and butter in double boiler. Beat eggs, add sugar, chocolate and butter mixture and vanilla extract, then add dry ingredients. Pour batter into 9" x 13" pan. Bake 50 minutes.

When cake is cool, frost with either Rich Chocolate Frosting or Chocolate Fudge Frosting.

Cherokee Park Chocolate Cake

Preparation time: 30 minutes
Baking time: 45 minutes

2	cups sugar	2	teaspoons baking soda
½	cup butter or margarine	½	teaspoon salt
2	eggs, well beaten	1	teaspoon vanilla extract
2	squares unsweetened chocolate, melted	1	cup buttermilk
2½	cups cake flour, sifted	¾	cup warm water

Preheat oven to 350°.

Cream the sugar and butter. Add eggs and chocolate. Mix in dry ingredients, alternating with the milk. Lastly, add warm water very gently. Bake in 350° oven about 45 minutes. Bake in 9" x 13" cake pan or two 9" layer pans. If baking in layers, test after 25 minutes and remove from oven if fork or straw comes out clean.

When cake is cool frost with Rich Chocolate Frosting or Chocolate Fudge Frosting.

Rich Chocolate Frosting

Preparation time: 15 minutes

½	**cup butter**
2	**squares unsweetened chocolate, melted**
2	**cups powdered sugar**
2	**tablespoons cream**
1	**teaspoon vanilla extract**

Beat together until smooth. Add more cream if necessary. Spread on cooled cake.

Chocolate Fudge Frosting

Preparation time: 15 minutes

2	**cups sugar**
3	**squares unsweetened chocolate**
½	**cup butter or margarine**
½	**cup milk**

Mix together and boil rapidly for 2 minutes. Cool and beat.

 The Ringling Bros.' big change in 1890 from travel by circus wagon to transport by rail spurred dramatic growth for the Circus. America's rapidly expanding rail system enabled them to cover greater distances and reach larger cities in record time. By 1891, the Circus had grown from one tent to a spectacular three-ring circus. As their success grew, so did their string of rail cars, which totaled an amazing 83 cars by 1918. By 1933, the Circus reportedly steamed into New York with 100 clowns, 735 horses, and hundreds of wild animals to perform before an audience of 10,000.

Arcadia Carrot Cake

Preparation time: 45 minutes
Baking time: 1 hour 10 minutes

Cake
3	cups sifted flour
2½	cups sugar
2	teaspoons baking powder
2	teaspoons cinnamon
1	teaspoon baking soda
½	teaspoon salt
2	large eggs
1½	cups vegetable oil
2	cups grated carrots
1	cup crushed pineapple, not drained
1	cup chopped pecans
2	teaspoons vanilla extract

Frosting
2	cups powdered sugar
½	cup butter, softened
1	3-ounce package cream cheese
	lemon juice

Preheat oven to 350°.

For cake, sift together dry ingredients and set aside.

Beat eggs until thick and lemon colored. Add vegetable oil and continue beating. Add carrots, pineapple, pecans and vanilla extract. Add dry ingredients and mix thoroughly. Pour into a buttered and floured Bundt pan. Bake 1 hour 10 minutes.

For frosting, cream butter, sugar and cream cheese. Add enough lemon juice so frosting is easy to spread when cake is cool.

Baroque Blueberry Cake

Preparation time: 30 minutes
Baking time: 1 hour

Cake
½	cup butter or margarine
1¼	cups brown sugar
2	large eggs, beaten
1	teaspoon baking soda in 3 tablespoons milk
1	pint blueberries, washed
1½	cups sifted flour

Hard Sauce
½	cup butter
1½	cups powdered sugar
1	teaspoon vanilla extract

Preheat oven to 350°.

For cake, cream butter and sugar. Add remaining ingredients. Stir well.

Bake in 9" square lightly greased pan for 1 hour.

For hard sauce, blend all ingredients until smooth.

Serve over warm blueberry cake.

———————•·•·•·•———————

 In the young Ringling Bros. Circus, John Ringling's job was to handle the scheduling and make circus bookings and arrangements in selected towns and cities. His keen business sense and ability to appraise opportunities enabled him to choose the most prosperous and receptive towns along their route.

———————•·•·•·•———————

Cape Coral Cranberry Shortcake

Preparation time: 45 minutes

Baking time: 45 minutes

Makes 1 pound shortcake

Shortcake

2	cups flour
1½	cups sugar
2	teaspoons baking powder
½	teaspoon salt
4	tablespoons butter or margarine
1	cup milk
3	cups cranberries, washed and halved

Butter Sauce

1	cup butter
1	cup sugar
1	cup brown sugar
1	cup cream
	dash of salt

Preheat oven to 375°.

For shortcake, sift flour, sugar, baking powder and salt into mixing bowl. Mix in softened butter. Add milk and cranberries which have been slightly dusted with flour. Bake in greased 9" x 13" cake pan for 45 minutes.

Combine all the ingredients for the butter sauce in double boiler over medium heat for 25 - 30 minutes, stirring occasionally. Serve on top of shortcake.

For a smaller recipe, halve all ingredients.

Roman Rhubarb Cake

Preparation time: 30 minutes
Baking time: 1 hour

Makes 9" x 13" cake, about 16 - 20 pieces

Cake
1½	cups light brown sugar
½	cup butter or margarine
1	large egg
1	cup sour milk
1	teaspoon baking soda
2	cups flour, sifted
1	teaspoon vanilla extract
1½	cups raw rhubarb, finely chopped

Topping
½	cup sugar
1	teaspoon cinnamon

Preheat oven to 325°.

In a large mixing bowl, cream sugar and butter. Add egg. Mix baking soda and sour milk together and add to sugar mixture. Sift flour and stir into above mixture. Stir in rhubarb. Place batter in baking pan. In a small bowl mix topping ingredients together and sprinkle over batter.

Bake 1 hour in a greased and floured 9" x 13" cake pan.

When the Ringling brothers bought out their biggest rival in 1906, becoming the Ringling Bros. and Barnum & Bailey Circus, their profits catapulted. Their Circus became dominant in the industry and grew toward a monopoly unrestrained by government regulation.

Casey Key Cheese Cake

Preparation time: 30 minutes
Baking time: 35 - 40 minutes

Makes 9" cake

2	8-ounce packages cream cheese
2	large eggs
1	cup sugar
½	teaspoon salt
1	teaspoon vanilla extract
1	9" graham cracker pie shell
½	cup sour cream

Preheat oven to 300°.

Beat cheese, eggs, ¾ cup sugar, salt and vanilla until smooth. Pour into pie shell. Bake 35 - 45 minutes. Chill. Mix together sour cream and ¼ cup sugar. Spread on top of pie when chilled.

Gondola Gold Cake

Preparation time: 20 minutes
Baking time: 40 - 45 minutes

Serves 12 - 14

10 - 12	large egg yolks
1	large egg
1	cup plus 2 tablespoons sugar
1¼	cups cake flour
3	teaspoons baking powder
1	teaspoon vanilla extract
	dash of salt
½	cup lukewarm water

Preheat oven to 350°.

In electric mixer, beat yolks, egg and sugar until very thick. Add remaining ingredients and mix well. Pour into an angel food pan. Bake 40 - 45 minutes.

187

Medieval Faire Gingerbread Muffins

Preparation time: 20 minutes
Baking time: 1 hour

Makes 12 cakes

2	large eggs
1	cup sugar
1	cup dark molasses
2	teaspoons ginger
1	teaspoon cinnamon
	pinch of salt
1	cup boiling water
2	teaspoons baking soda, dissolved in water
3	cups sifted flour

Preheat oven to 350°.

Beat sugar and eggs together. Add molasses, ginger, cinnamon and salt. Add water and flour alternately. Pour batter into 12 muffin tins. Bake 1 hour.

This is an old fashioned heavy gingerbread. Delicious topped with whipped heavy cream or lemon sauce.

———••●●••———

The early Ringling Bros. Circus included a variety of domestic animals, including dogs, geese and birds. It wasn't until later that wild animals such as the great elephants and tigers moved into the spotlight. Always a cautious man, John Ringling was concerned about problems the big cats might bring, and he eventually dropped these thrilling acts from the show.

When Sarasota, Florida became home base for the Circus in 1927, Ringling began making plans for a permanent, large scale zoological park. And so, the wild animals again drew audiences' cheers.

———••●●••———

Prohibition Rum Cake

Preparation time: 45 minutes

Baking time: 1 hour

Serves 12

Cake
1	box yellow cake mix
1	package vanilla instant pudding
½	cup water
½	cup light rum
½	cup cooking oil
4	large eggs

First Glaze
½	cup butter or margarine
1	cup sugar
¼	cup water
¼	cup light rum

Second Glaze
½	package powdered sugar
¼	cup light rum
¼	teaspoon salt

Preheat oven to 300°.

To make cake, mix first 6 ingredients well and beat lightly until blended. Bake 1 hour in angel food cake pan.

For first glaze, boil butter, sugar, water and rum together for 3 minutes. Pour over hot cake in pan. Remove cake from the pan.

For second glaze, mix powdered sugar, rum and salt together. Drizzle mixture over cake.

Sunshine Coast Sponge Cake

Preparation time: 30 minutes
Baking time: 50 minutes

Serves 12 - 14

Cake
12	egg yolks
1⅛	cups sugar
1¼	cups sifted cake flour
¼	teaspoon salt
3	level teaspoons baking powder
1	teaspoon vanilla extract
½	cup boiling water

Caramel Icing
¼	cup butter or margarine
1	cup light brown sugar
¼	cup milk
1½	cups powdered sugar
1	teaspoon vanilla extract

Preheat oven to 325°.

For cake, beat egg yolks with electric mixer until thick and lemon colored. Beat in sugar gradually. Add vanilla, sifted flour, baking powder and salt. Carefully fold in boiling water.

Bake 50 minutes in a greased and floured 9" x 13" cake pan.

For icing, combine butter and sugar and boil 2 minutes. Add milk and boil 1 minute more. Cool. Stir in powdered sugar and vanilla. Spread on cooled cake.

Cookies & Candy

Aunt Ruth's Lace Cookies

Preparation time: 20 minutes
Baking time: 8 minutes

Makes 2 dozen

1	cup quick cooking oats	¼	teaspoon baking powder
1	cup sugar	½	cup unsalted butter or margarine, melted
2	tablespoons plus 1 teaspoon flour	1	large egg, lightly beaten
1½	teaspoons salt	2	teaspoons vanilla extract

Preheat oven to 325°.

Combine dry ingredients in a mixing bowl. Using electric mixer, add melted butter, beaten egg and vanilla, and blend on medium speed. Drop cookie mixture in small amounts on 11" x 17" x 1" cookie sheet lined with parchment paper. Bake 8 minutes.

Remove parchment paper from baking sheet to cool cookies.

All-Night Meringue Cookies

Preparation time: 15 minutes
Standing time: 4 - 6 hours or overnight

Makes 2 dozen

2	egg whites, room temperature	½	pound chocolate, mint or butterscotch morsels
⅔	cup sugar		
	pinch of salt	⅓	cup nuts, finely chopped (optional)
½	teaspoon vanilla extract or mint flavoring		food coloring (optional)

Preheat oven to 375°.

Using electric mixer, beat egg whites into stiff peaks. Continue beating and slowly add sugar. Add a pinch of salt and vanilla extract. Fold in chocolate morsels. Nuts and food coloring may be added if desired. Drop by spoonfuls onto baking sheet lined with parchment paper. Place in oven and immediately turn oven off. Leave in oven 4 - 6 hours or overnight.

Lemon Bonbon Cookies

Preparation time: 30 minutes   Makes 2 dozen
Baking time: 10 minutes

Cookies
1	cup unsalted butter or margarine, softened
⅓	cup powdered sugar, sifted
2	cups flour

Frosting
1	cup powdered sugar
2	tablespoons fresh lemon juice
1	teaspoon unsalted butter or margarine, melted
½	teaspoon grated lemon zest

Preheat oven to 375°.

For cookie mixture, using an electric mixer on medium speed, blend butter and sugar. Slowly add flour.

With floured hands, roll into 1" balls. Place on cookie sheet 1" apart and gently flatten to ½" thickness with a small glass or cookie press. Bake 10 minutes.

For frosting, blend powdered sugar, lemon juice, butter and lemon zest until smooth and creamy.

When cookies are cool, frost half of them. Top with remaining cookies.

The sideshows of the Ringling Bros. Circus were conceived to entertain early arrivals before they entered the menagerie or the big top. The bearded lady, the sword swallower, the human skeleton, and Chang-Eng, the Siamese twins are just a few of the legendary sideshow personalities that entertained audiences with their curious displays.

Snowbird Molasses Cookies

Preparation time: 30 minutes
Baking time: 10 - 12 minutes

Makes 4 dozen

2	rounded cups flour	1	cup sugar
2	teaspoons baking soda	¾	cup shortening
1	teaspoon ground cinnamon	1	large egg
1	teaspoon ground ginger	4	tablespoons molasses
1	teaspoon ground cloves	½	cup sugar for dipping
½	teaspoon salt		

Preheat oven to 350°.

Sift together flour, baking soda, cinnamon and salt. Add ginger and cloves. Set aside. Using electric mixer, cream sugar and shortening together. Add egg, beating to blend. Add molasses and mix to blend. Slowly add dry ingredients while mixing on low speed. With floured hands, roll into 1" balls, dip one side in sugar, and place 1" apart on cookie sheet. Bake 10 - 12 minutes. Cool on wire rack.

Punta Gorda Peanut Butter Cookies

Preparation time: 30 minutes
Baking time: 10 - 12 minutes

Makes 4 dozen

1½	cups flour	½	cup sugar
½	teaspoon baking soda	½	cup dark brown sugar, firmly packed
½	teaspoon salt	1	large egg
½	cup shortening less 2 teaspoons	½	teaspoon vanilla extract
½	cup creamy peanut butter	½	cup sugar for sprinkling

Preheat oven to 375°.

Sift together flour, baking soda and salt. Using electric mixer, cream shortening, peanut butter and sugars until blended. Add egg and vanilla and blend on medium speed. Slowly add dry ingredients and mix until blended. With floured hands, form into 1" balls and roll in sugar. Place on cookie sheet 1" apart. Gently press with tines of a fork. Bake 10 - 12 minutes. Cool on wire rack.

Wally's Oatmeal Cookies

Preparation time: 30 minutes
Baking time: 10 - 12 minutes

Makes 5 dozen

1½	**cups flour**
1	**teaspoon salt**
1	**teaspoon baking soda**
3	**cups quick cooking oats**
1	**cup shortening**
1	**cup dark brown sugar, firmly packed**
1	**cup sugar**
2	**large eggs**
1	**teaspoon vanilla extract**
½	**cup pecans, coarsely chopped (optional)**

Preheat oven to 375°.

Sift together flour, salt and baking soda. Add oats. Set aside.

Using electric mixer, cream shortening and sugars until blended. Add eggs and vanilla and blend on medium speed. Slowly add dry ingredients with mixer on medium low. Stir in nuts.

Drop by rounded teaspoonfuls onto cookie sheet about 1" apart.

Bake 10 - 12 minutes. Transfer to wire rack to cool.

—··•••··—

*A popular 20th-century American painting in The John and Mable Ringling Museum of Art is the 1930 **Wonderland Circus Sideshow, Coney Island** by Reginald Marsh. It presents a crowded "pyramid" of steamy, pleasure-seeking figures in a composition reminiscent of Peter Paul Rubens.*

—··•••··—

Sarasota Snowballs

Preparation Time: 20 minutes
Baking time: 20 minutes

Makes 3 dozen

2	cups cake flour	1	teaspoon vanilla extract
1	cup unsalted butter or margarine, softened	¾	cup pecans, finely chopped
1	cup powdered sugar, sifted		

Preheat oven to 300°.

Using electric mixer, blend flour, butter, ½ cup sugar and vanilla extract. Stir in nuts. With floured hands, roll into 1" balls. Place 1" apart on cookie sheet. Bake 20 minutes. Do not brown.

Dust with remaining powdered sugar. Transfer to wire rack to cool.

Scottish Cookies

Preparation time: 1 hour
Baking time: 18 - 20 minutes

Makes 2½ dozen

1	cup unsalted butter or margarine, softened
1	cup powdered sugar, sifted
1½	teaspoons vanilla extract
2	cups flour, sifted
⅔	cup almonds, finely chopped

Preheat oven to 350°.

Using electric mixer, beat butter, ½ cup sugar and vanilla on medium speed until blended. Slowly add flour until well mixed. Stir in nuts.

For ease of rolling out, chill dough 20 minutes in refrigerator. Roll out dough between 2 sheets of waxed paper to ¼" thickness. Using cookie cutter, cut dough into desired shapes. Place ½" apart on ungreased cookie sheet. Bake 18 - 20 minutes. Remove from oven and cool 1 minute. Sprinkle with remaining powdered sugar. Transfer to wire rack to cool.

Treasure Island Powdered Sugar Cookies

Preparation time: 30 minutes
Refrigeration time: 2 - 3 hours
Baking time: 12 - 15 minutes

Makes 4 dozen

2¼	cups flour
1	cup powdered sugar
½	teaspoon salt
½	teaspoon cream of tartar
½	teaspoon baking soda
1	cup unsalted butter or margarine, softened
1	large egg
½	teaspoon vanilla extract
½	cup sugar for dipping

Preheat oven to 350°.

Sift together flour, powdered sugar, salt, cream of tartar and baking soda.

Using electric mixer, blend butter, egg and vanilla. With mixer on low speed, slowly add dry ingredients and mix until dough begins to pull away from side of bowl.

Wrap dough in waxed paper and refrigerate for 2 - 3 hours.

With floured hands, roll into 1" balls. Place 1" apart on cookie sheet. Gently press dough, using the bottom of a small drinking glass dipped in sugar.

Bake 12 - 15 minutes. Transfer to wire rack to cool.

———————•••••———————

 Clowns have entertained circus fans since the 18th century. Wearing white, often sad-faced make up and tattered, baggy clothes, performers such as the great Emmett Kelly, known to millions as "Weary Willie," drew cheers and laughter from Ringling Bros. and Barnum & Bailey audiences.

———————•••••———————

Naples Nut Cookies

Preparation time: 30 minutes   Makes 6 dozen
Baking time: 10 - 12 minutes

1½	cups brazil nuts, coarsely chopped
1	cup hazelnuts or almonds, coarsely chopped
½	cup pecans or walnuts, chopped
1¼	cups pitted dates, chopped
1¼	cups dried apricots, chopped
1¼	cups flour
½	teaspoon each baking soda and baking powder
½	teaspoon cinnamon
¼	teaspoon salt
½	cup unsalted butter or margarine
¾	cup brown sugar, firmly packed
1	large egg

Preheat oven to 350°.

Mix nuts and fruits with ¼ cup flour. Set aside.

Sift together remaining flour, baking soda, baking powder, cinnamon and salt. Using electric mixer, blend butter and brown sugar until light and creamy. Beat in egg. Add dry ingredients, mixing until smooth. Stir in fruit and nut mixture.

Drop by rounded teaspoonfuls 1½" apart onto a greased cookie sheet. Bake for 10 - 12 minutes or until lightly browned. Transfer to wire rack to cool.

A beloved attraction of the Ringling Bros. and Barnum & Bailey Circus, a young Australian teenager by the name of May Wirth was reputed to be the greatest equestrienne of all-time. May's great crowd pleaser was to leap onto a running horse, while her feet were firmly planted in market baskets. May and her adoptive, equestrian parents were the highest paid act in the show.

Rolled Sugar Cookies

Preparation time: 40 minutes
Refrigeration time: 30 minutes
Baking time: 8 - 10 minutes

Makes 5 dozen

½	cup unsalted butter or margarine	2	tablespoons baking powder
1	cup sugar	1¾	cups flour
1	large egg	1	egg white, beaten stiff

Using electric mixer, cream butter and sugar together. Add whole egg and beat until creamy. Sift baking powder and flour together and add to mixture. Fold in beaten egg white. Refrigerate dough for at least 30 minutes.

Preheat oven to 350°. Using a floured rolling pin, roll out a portion of the dough on a floured board to a thickness of ⅛". Cut out with a cookie cutter. Place 1½" apart on lightly greased cookie sheet. Bake 8 - 10 minutes or until cookies are slightly brown. Transfer to wire rack to cool.

Manasota Chocolate Macaroons

Preparation time: 20 minutes
Baking time: 25 minutes

Makes 70 small macaroons

4	egg whites	½	pound semisweet chocolate morsels
½	teaspoon salt	1	cup broken walnuts
¼	teaspoon cream of tartar	1	teaspoon vanilla extract
1½	cups sugar		

Preheat oven to 300°.

Using electric mixer, beat egg whites until foamy. Add salt and cream of tartar, beating until whites are stiff enough to hold peaks, but not dry. Add sugar, 2 tablespoons at a time, beating thoroughly after each addition. By hand, gently fold in chocolate, nuts and vanilla. Drop by teaspoonfuls onto a baking sheet covered with parchment paper. Bake for 25 minutes. Remove macaroons from paper while still slightly warm. Cool on wire rack.

Venetian Biscotti

Preparation time: 1 hour
Baking time: 40 minutes

Makes 24 biscuits

½	cup slivered almonds
⅓	cup unsalted butter or margarine
¾	cup sugar
2	large eggs
1	teaspoon vanilla extract
½	teaspoon almond extract
1½	teaspoons grated orange zest
2¼	cups flour
½	teaspoon baking powder
⅛	teaspoon ground nutmeg
¼	teaspoon salt
½	cup candied ginger, coarsely chopped

Preheat oven to 325°.

Roast almonds until golden, about 8 minutes. Set aside.

Using electric mixer, cream butter and sugar until light and creamy. Add eggs, vanilla extract, almond extract and orange zest and blend on medium speed. Set aside.

In a separate bowl, sift together flour, baking powder, nutmeg and salt. Add to creamed mixture and blend well. Stir in almonds and ginger. Shape dough into 2 logs ½" high, 1½" wide and 12" long. Place 2" apart on greased, floured baking sheet. Bake 25 - 30 minutes until golden brown. Transfer to wire rack to cool, about 8 minutes.

Place logs on a cutting board and slice at a 45° angle into ½" slices. Lay slices flat on baking sheet and return to oven for 20 minutes, 10 minutes on each side. Transfer to wire rack to cool.

Store at room temperature in a tightly covered container.

Biscotti come from Italy where they are traditionally dunked into coffee or wine. Difficult to bite, they soften to a pleasing texture when dunked.

Palmetto Pecan Tassies

Preparation time: 30 minutes
Chilling time: 1 hour
Baking time: 20 minutes

Makes 2 dozen

Pastry
1	**3-ounce package cream cheese, softened**
½	**cup unsalted butter or margarine, softened**
1¼	**cups flour**

Filling
1	**large egg, beaten**
¾	**cup brown sugar**
1	**tablespoon unsalted butter or margarine, melted**
½	**teaspoon vanilla**
½	**cup pecans, chopped**

Using electric mixer, blend cream cheese and butter. Slowly add flour until well blended. Place dough in plastic wrap and chill 1 hour in refrigerator.

Preheat oven to 350°.

For filling, using electric mixer, blend egg, sugar, butter and vanilla. Stir in pecans.

Remove dough from refrigerator. Shape chilled dough into 2 dozen 1" balls. Press into ungreased miniature muffin cups. Spoon filling into cups until ¾ full. Bake 20 minutes. Cool and serve.

These freeze well.

Always ready to amuse the circus crowds, clowns were kept close at hand in Clown Alley, a narrow enclave at the performers' entrance to the big top. In the event of a crisis—an escaped animal or a violent summer storm—the clowns were ready to divert attention and calm the crowd.

Cinnamon Star Cookies

Preparation time: 1 hour
Refrigeration time: overnight
Baking time: 8 minutes

Makes 2 dozen

6	egg whites
1	pound dark brown sugar
2	tablespoons cinnamon
1	pound unblanched almonds, ground finely
1	cup powdered sugar
12	blanched almonds, sliced in half

Stir eggs for 20 minutes (do not beat) with brown sugar and cinnamon. Reserve 4 tablespoons of the mixture for topping. Add almonds. Let stand overnight in refrigerator.

Bring to room temperature, then stir in ½ cup powdered sugar.

Preheat oven to 300°.

Put ¼ of the dough on bread board covered with remaining powdered sugar. Turn several times dusting with powdered sugar. Roll out with rolling pin. Using a star cookie cutter dipped in powdered sugar, cut into stars. Repeat for remaining dough.

Grease cookie sheet with butter, then dust with flour. Put stars on sheet, top with small amount of reserved mixture and ½ blanched almond.

Bake 8 minutes. Allow to cool on cookie sheet.

Everyone loves the melodic, joyful music of the circus played on the instrument known as the calliope. The early steam operated calliope was always featured in the parade that led an eager crowd to the circus grounds. Later, it was replaced by the safer air operated calliope.

Holiday Fruit & Nut Cookies

Preparation time: 30 minutes
Refrigeration time: overnight
Baking time: 20 minutes

Makes 6 dozen

1	cup walnuts, coarsely chopped
1	cup whole pecans
1	cup whole hazelnuts
2	pounds dates, chopped
½	pound raisins
½	pound candied cherries, chopped
½	pound candied pineapple, chopped
2½	cups flour
1	teaspoon baking soda
1	teaspoon salt
1	cup unsalted butter or margarine, softened
1½	cups brown sugar
2	large eggs
1	teaspoon vanilla extract
½ - 1	cup brandy

Combine nuts and fruits in a large bowl. Set aside.

Sift together flour, baking soda and salt.

Using electric mixer, beat butter and sugar until creamy. Add eggs one at a time until well blended. With mixer on low, add sifted mixture. Add vanilla and brandy. Stir in fruit and nut mixture. Cover and refrigerate overnight.

Preheat oven to 325°.

Drop by teaspoonfuls onto lightly greased cookie sheet 1" apart. Bake 20 minutes. Transfer to wire rack to cool.

Cherry Christmas Cookies

Preparation time: 30 minutes
Baking time: 20 minutes

Makes 5 dozen

½	cup unsalted butter or margarine	1½	teaspoons grated lemon zest
¼	cup sugar	1	tablespoon lemon juice
1	large egg, separated	1¼	cups flour
½	teaspoon vanilla extract	½	cup walnuts or pecans, chopped fine
1	tablespoon grated orange zest		candied or maraschino cherries

Preheat oven to 350°.

Using electric mixer, cream butter and sugar together. Add egg yolk and blend well. Add vanilla, orange zest, lemon zest and lemon juice. Mix in flour. With floured hands, roll into 1" balls. Dip top of each ball in slightly beaten egg white and then into nuts. Place balls 1½" apart on cookie sheet. Press a cherry in the center top, flattening the ball slightly. Bake 20 minutes. Cool on wire rack.

Gram's Spritz Cookies

Preparation time: 30 minutes
Chilling time: 1 hour
Baking time: 7 - 10 minutes

Makes 4 dozen

1	cup unsalted butter, softened	2½	cups flour
⅔	cup sugar	⅛	teaspoon baking powder
3	large egg yolks	⅛	teaspoon salt
1	teaspoon almond extract		sprinkles (optional)

Preheat oven to 350°.

Sift together flour, baking powder and salt. Cream butter and sugar together with spoon. Blend in egg yolks one at a time. Add almond extract. Blend in dry ingredients. Divide mixture into 4 equal parts and shape into logs that fit your cookie press tube. Using desired cookie press shape, fill tube with dough. Follow cookie press instructions for shaping cookies. Coat cookies with sprinkles if desired. Bake on lightly greased cookie sheet 7 - 10 minutes. Transfer to wire rack to cool.

Tampa Bay Brownies

Preparation time: 20 minutes

Baking time: 25 minutes

Makes 24 squares

Brownies
½	cup unsalted butter or margarine
1	cup sugar
4	large eggs
1	cup flour
1	16-ounce can chocolate syrup
½	cup nuts, chopped

Frosting
1⅓	cups sugar
6	tablespoons milk
6	tablespoons unsalted butter or margarine
½	cup semisweet chocolate morsels
½	teaspoon vanilla extract

Preheat oven to 350°.

Using electric mixer, cream butter and sugar together. Add eggs and blend. Add flour and chocolate syrup. Stir in nuts. Do not over mix.

Spread mixture in lightly greased 15½" x 10½" x 1" jelly-roll pan. Bake 25 minutes. Do not over bake. Brownies will be moist in center. Cool before frosting.

For frosting, combine sugar, milk and butter in a small saucepan over medium heat. Bring slowly to a boil and boil for 30 seconds. Turn burner off and add chocolate morsels, stirring until melted. Stir in vanilla extract.

Using a rubber spatula, spread frosting evenly over brownies.

Sarasota Quay Cocoa Brownies

Preparation time: 20 minutes
Baking time: 25 - 30 minutes

Makes 16 squares

4	tablespoons cocoa powder		1	cup flour
1½	cups brown sugar		¼	teaspoon salt
½	cup vegetable oil		¾	cup pecans, chopped
1	large egg or egg substitute		1	teaspoon vanilla extract
1	egg white			

Preheat oven to 350°.

Using electric mixer on medium speed, combine ingredients in the order listed. Pour into greased 7" x 11" x 2" pan. Bake 25 - 30 minutes, or until toothpick inserted in center comes out clean. Cool before cutting into serving pieces.

Scottish Shortbread

Preparation time: 30 minutes
Baking time: 50 minutes

Makes 32 pieces

1	cup unsalted butter or margarine		1	tablespoon cornstarch
8	tablespoons sugar		1	teaspoon almond extract
2	cups flour			

Preheat oven to 300°.

Cream cool butter and sugar together. Sift flour and cornstarch together and slowly add to butter and sugar mixture. Add extract and blend ingredients together until smooth. Divide the dough into two equal parts and place each half on a greased 9" pie pan. Press mixture into the pans, spreading evenly. Mark dough in each pan into 16 pie-shaped pieces with the back of a knife. Prick dough with fork.

Bake for 50 minutes or until very light brown. Remove from oven and cut immediately into the marked pie pieces. Cool and store in a tightly covered container.

Crème de Menthe Chocolate Bars

Preparation time: 40 minutes

Baking time: 25 - 30 minutes

Makes 24 squares

Bars
4	ounces unsweetened baking chocolate
1	cup unsalted butter or margarine
4	large eggs
2	cups sugar
1	cup flour, sifted
1	teaspoon vanilla extract
½	teaspoon salt

Filling
½	cup unsalted butter or margarine
2	cups powdered sugar, sifted
3	tablespoons white crème de menthe

Topping
6	ounces semisweet chocolate morsels
3	tablespoons water
4	tablespoons unsalted butter or margarine

Preheat oven to 350°.

For bars, melt baking chocolate and butter in a double boiler. Remove from heat and cool slightly. Set aside. Beat eggs until light. Gradually add sugar, then flour, vanilla, salt and melted chocolate. Beat 1 minute. Bake in a lightly greased 9" x 13" baking pan 25 - 30 minutes, until toothpick inserted in center comes out clean. Remove and cool.

For filling, beat together butter, sugar and crème de menthe. Mixture should be light and creamy. Using rubber spatula, spread over chocolate base. Chill 1½ hours.

For topping, in a double boiler melt ingredients, stirring frequently. Cool slightly. Using rubber spatula, spread over bars. This freezes well.

Heavenly Dream Bars

Preparation time: 30 minutes

Baking time: 50 minutes

Makes 24 bars

Crust
- ½ cup unsalted butter or margarine
- 1 cup flour

Filling
- 2 large eggs
- 1½ cups brown sugar
- ½ teaspoon salt
- ½ cup shredded coconut
- 1 cup walnuts, finely chopped

Frosting
- 1½ cups powdered sugar
- 2 tablespoons unsalted butter or margarine, softened
- 2 - 3 tablespoons orange juice
- 1 teaspoon almond extract

Preheat oven to 350°.

For crust, using electric mixer, beat butter until creamy. Add flour and mix on low speed until crumbly. Pat crumbs firmly into the bottom of greased and floured 9" square cake pan. Bake 10 minutes. Remove from oven and cool slightly.

For filling, beat eggs, then mix in brown sugar and salt. Fold in coconut and walnuts. Spread over baked crust and bake 30 minutes longer. Cool.

For frosting, using electric mixer, cream powdered sugar and butter together. Add orange juice and almond extract. Spread frosting on cool bars.

Chocolate Coconut Party Bars

Preparation time: 15 minutes
Baking time: 30 minutes

Makes 24 bars

½	cup unsalted butter or margarine	1	cup flaked coconut
1½	cups graham cracker crumbs	1	cup walnuts, chopped
1½	cups semisweet chocolate morsels	1	can sweetened condensed milk

Preheat oven to 325°.

Melt butter or margarine in a 9" x 13" x 2" baking pan. Sprinkle graham cracker crumbs evenly over butter. Add layer of chocolate morsels, spread evenly. Repeat this step with coconut and walnuts. Pour sweetened condensed milk over the top.

Bake for 30 minutes. Cool before cutting.

Tidy Island Toffee Nut Bars

Preparation time: 15 minutes
Baking time: 15 - 20 minutes

Makes 48 bars

½	cup unsalted butter or margarine	2	cups flour
½	cup shortening	½	teaspoon salt
1	cup dark brown sugar, packed	6	ounces semisweet chocolate morsels
1	egg yolk	1	cup nuts, finely chopped
1	teaspoon vanilla extract		

Preheat oven to 350°.

Using electric mixer, beat butter and shortening for 30 seconds. Add brown sugar and beat until fluffy. Add egg yolk, salt and vanilla. Mix well. Gradually add flour until blended. Press evenly into ungreased 17" x 11" x 1" jelly-roll pan. Bake until light brown, about 15 - 20 minutes.

While still warm, sprinkle chocolate morsels over crust using a rubber spatula to spread evenly. Sprinkle with nuts. Cool and cut into bars.

Luscious Lemon Bars

Preparation time: 30 minutes
Baking time: 45 minutes

Makes 16 bars

Crust
1	cup flour
¼	cup powdered sugar
½	cup unsalted butter or margarine

Filling
2	large eggs, lightly beaten
1	cup sugar
2	tablespoons fresh lemon juice
1	teaspoon grated lemon zest
½	teaspoon baking powder
¼	teaspoon salt
¼ - ½	cup powdered sugar, sifted, for dusting

Preheat oven to 350°.

In medium sized mixing bowl, combine flour and powdered sugar. Using a pastry blender cut in butter or margarine until mixture is crumbly. Gently pat crumbly mixture evenly into bottom of lightly greased 8" square cake pan.

Bake 20 minutes or until lightly colored at edge of pastry. Remove from oven. Cool.

For filling, beat eggs. Add remaining filling ingredients. Stir until well blended. Pour over cooled crust. Return to oven. Bake 25 minutes.

Dust with powdered sugar while still warm. Cool before slicing.

Magic Mixed Nut Bars

Preparation time: 30 minutes
Baking time: 20 minutes

Makes 24 bars

1½	cups flour
¾	cup dark brown sugar, packed
1	teaspoon salt
½	cup chilled unsalted butter or margarine, cut into 1" pieces
6	ounces butterscotch morsels
½	cup white corn syrup
2	tablespoons unsalted butter or margarine
1	pound salted mixed nuts

Preheat oven to 350°.

Combine flour, sugar and salt in medium mixing bowl. Cut chilled butter into flour mixture using pastry blender until mixture is crumbly. Press evenly into greased 9" x 13" x 2" baking pan.

Bake 10 minutes. Remove from oven. Cool.

Meanwhile, melt butterscotch morsels, corn syrup and butter in a saucepan over medium low heat, stirring frequently. Remove from heat.

Spread mixed nuts evenly over baked crust. Drizzle with melted morsel mixture. Return to oven. Bake 10 minutes. Remove and cool slightly. Cut while still warm.

———•••••———

 The Ringling Bros. and Barnum & Bailey Circus has brought us countless, sensational acts over the years. An early favorite featured human projectiles Hugo and Vittorio Zacchini, who were the concluding act at each performance. One or both were shot into flight from a cannon to make their thrilling net landing at the end of the big top.

———•••••———

Mistletoe Divinity

Preparation time: 1 hour   Makes 40 pieces

2	cups sugar		2	egg whites
½	cup light corn syrup		1	teaspoon vanilla extract
½	cup water			pinch of salt

In a heavy two-quart saucepan, stir together sugar, water and syrup. Stir over medium-high heat until sugar dissolves and mixture boils, about 5 - 7 minutes. Boil slowly over moderately high heat until a candy thermometer shows 260° or a small amount of syrup dropped in cold water forms a hard ball, about 15 minutes.

Using electric mixer on medium speed, beat egg whites until stiff peaks form. Slowly pour hot syrup over egg whites, beating on high speed. Add vanilla. Continue to beat just until candy starts to lose its gloss, about 5 minutes.

Drop candy from spoon onto waxed paper. Candy will mound into a soft shape. Cool. Store tightly covered.

Decadent Chocolate Fudge

Preparation time: 1½ hours   Makes 16 pieces

2	cups sugar		2	tablespoons butter
½	cup milk			dash of salt
¼	cup cream		1	teaspoon vanilla
2	squares unsweetened chocolate		½	cup nuts, coarsely chopped

Butter the sides of a heavy two-quart saucepan. Combine sugar, milk, cream and chocolate. Stir over medium-high heat until sugar dissolves and mixture boils. Boil slowly over medium low heat until a candy thermometer shows 234° or a small amount of syrup dropped in cold water forms a soft ball. Remove from heat. Add butter and vanilla but do not stir. Cool to lukewarm, about 50 minutes.

Add nuts. Beat vigorously about 7 minutes or until fudge becomes very thick and just starts to lose its gloss. Spread in a buttered 8" square cake pan. Cool. Cut when firm.

Tampico Penuche

Preparation time: 1 hour   Makes 16 squares

3	**cups light brown sugar**
⅓	**cup cream**
½	**cup milk**
	pinch of salt
1	**tablespoon butter**
1	**teaspoon vanilla**
½	**cup walnuts or pecans, chopped**

Butter sides of a heavy two-quart saucepan. Combine sugar, cream, milk and salt. Cook over medium-high heat, stirring constantly, till sugar dissolves and mixture boils. Continue cooking over medium-low heat stirring only as necessary to prevent sticking, to 236° on a candy thermometer or until syrup can be shaped into a soft ball that flattens when removed from water.

Remove from heat and set saucepan in cold water. Add butter and vanilla but do not stir. Cool without stirring until lukewarm.

Beat vigorously until mixture begins to thicken. Add nuts. Continue beating till mixture becomes very thick and starts to lose its gloss, about 10 minutes.

Quickly pour into buttered 8" square cake pan. Chill in refrigerator until firm.

—··•●•··—

 Elephants dominate many of the Ringling families' favorite circus stories. One tale recalls when Fannie the elephant charged, sideswiping one of the Ringling women and sending her 15 feet in the air. Another story told of the time when an elephant ran into the kitchen of a nearby house and fell through the floor into the cistern. The great animal had to be lifted out with a derrick. There was never a dull moment at the circus.

—··•●•··—

Tamiami Toffee

Preparation time: 1 hour

Makes 2 pounds

2¼	cups sugar	1	cup butter
1	teaspoon salt	¾	cup almonds, finely chopped
½	cup water	9	ounces chocolate morsels

Butter sides of a heavy two-quart saucepan. Combine sugar, salt, water and butter. Cook over medium-high heat, stirring constantly, till sugar dissolves and mixture boils. Continue cooking over medium-low heat stirring occasionally, to 260° on a candy thermometer or until a small amount of syrup dropped in cold water forms a hard ball. Add almonds and continue cooking until thermometer reaches 300° or until a small amount of syrup forms a hard ball when dropped into cold water and is brittle when removed from water.

Quickly pour on warm, buttered cookie sheets. Melt chocolate morsels, and spread over toffee. Sprinkle with nuts. Cool and break into pieces.

Barnum & Bailey Peanut Brittle

Preparation time: 1 hour

Makes 2 pounds

2	cups sugar
⅔	cup light corn syrup
1	cup water
2	cups raw peanuts
1	teaspoon each salt and baking soda

Combine sugar, corn syrup and water in a heavy 3-quart saucepan. Stir over medium-high heat until sugar dissolves and mixture comes to a boil. Continue cooking over medium-low heat stirring occasionally, to 275° on a candy thermometer or until syrup separates into threads that are not hard or brittle. Add peanuts and salt and continue cooking, to 295°. Syrup should be a clear golden color.

Remove from heat. Quickly stir in baking soda. Spread as quickly and thinly as possible on a large buttered cookie sheet. Cool and break into pieces.

Lido Casino Candied Nuts

Preparation time: 30 minutes
Baking time: 30 minutes

Makes 1 pound

½	**cup butter**
2	**egg whites**
1	**cup sugar**
	dash of salt
3½	**cups walnuts or pecans**

Preheat oven to 325°.

Melt butter in oven in a large cake pan.

Using electric mixer, beat egg whites until stiff. Beat in sugar and salt.

Mix nuts with egg white mixture and pour in cake pan. Bake for 30 minutes, stirring every 10 minutes until butter is completely absorbed. Separate into clusters.

Cool. Store in airtight container.

Among the most memorable of the Ringling Bros. Circus performers was aerialist Lillian Leitzel. The feisty, petite Leitzel would swing high overhead on the roman rings, throwing her body over her shoulder more than 100 times. Asked once if she had been married before, the bright, charismatic performer replied, "Yes, but I don't remember his name."

Healthy Substitutes & Seasonings

Healthy Substitutes

If the recipe calls for	Try
whole milk	skim milk
evaporated milk	evaporated skim milk
heavy cream or half-and-half cream	skim milk
whole milk cultured buttermilk	low-fat cultured buttermilk
sweetened whipped cream	nondairy whipped topping
sour cream	plain low-fat yogurt
fruit-flavored yogurt	plain low-fat yogurt plus fresh fruit
ice cream	ice milk, frozen yogurt
whole milk ricotta cheese	part-skim ricotta cheese
regular creamed cottage cheese	1% low-fat cottage cheese
cream cheese	light cream cheese, Neufchâtel cheese
Cheddar cheese	reduced-calorie Cheddar, part-skim mozzarella
flavored gelatin	unflavored gelatin plus unsweetened fruit juice
fruit jelly or jam	low-sugar fruit spread
frozen fruit, sweetened	fresh fruit, canned fruit in natural juices
canned fruit in syrup	fresh fruit, canned fruit in natural juices
mayonnaise	reduced-calorie mayonnaise
salad dressing	reduced-calorie dressing
fat used for frying or baking	vegetable cooking spray
greasing a pan	vegetable cooking spray
flour (for thickening)	cornstarch, arrowroot, potatoes
whole egg (for thickening)	flour (1 tablespoon = 1 egg)
whole egg (ingredient)	egg whites, egg substitute
canned tuna in oil	canned tuna in water
chicken with skin	chicken without skin
ground beef	ground turkey, ground chicken

Herbs and spices are delicious natural gifts to cooks. They can dramatically enhance the flavor of many dishes and provide excellent healthful substitutes when restricting the use of salt. There once was a time when spices were worth their weight in gold. Use your imagination and your meals will never be boring.

Kitchen Spices

The Spice	Its Flavor	Use it with. . .
Allspice	Slightly peppery	Meats, game, poultry and ham
Caraway	Spicy	Rich meats such as pork, duck and goose
Cinnamon	Slightly sweet	Meats, stews and curries
Cumin	Warm flavor	Curries, meat stews and sausages
Cloves	Strongly aromatic	Beef, lamb, pork stews and ham
Garlic	Aromatic and pungent	Beef, lamb, pork and stews
Ginger	Spicy	Meat and poultry stews
Paprika	Slightly piquant	Meat and poultry stews

Kitchen Herbs

The herb	Its Flavor	Use it with. . .
Basil	Sweet	Tomatoes, mushrooms, eggs, in salads
Chives	Onion	Eggs, sauces and salads
Dill	Aromatic	Cabbage, green beans, rice, cooked root vegetables
Marjoram	Delicate	Beans, eggplant
Rosemary	Pungent	Potatoes au gratin, stuffed vegetables
Savory	Peppery	Legumes, vegetable salads
Thyme	Aromatic	Sautéed or baked vegetables

Use a light hand when adding fresh herbs to microwave recipes because the flavor may be stronger than in conventional preparation.

Become a Member Today

As a member, share in the support of a cultural treasure like no other. The Ringling Museum is the largest art museum in the Southeast. In addition to the Art Museum, the estate includes Cà d'Zan, the fanciful, historic home of John and Mable Ringling; the Circus Museum filled with brightly painted wagons, glittering costumes and fascinating memorabilia; and the classical sculpture Courtyard amidst landscaped grounds. The Museum offers a stellar array of exhibitions, programs and events that put the art world spotlight on Sarasota. No wonder 255,000 people visited the Museum last year.

Museum members enjoy unlimited free admission; great exhibitions; educational programs; special openings; gallery talks; films; travel opportunities; and special discounts on Museum Shop purchases.

Join today and start enjoying the benefits only membership can provide.

To join the Ringling Museum of Art, check the membership level that's right for you, fill out this form and return it today to:

The John and Mable Ringling Museum of Art Foundation, Inc.
5401 Bay Shore Road, Sarasota, FL 34243
Attention: Jocelyn Stevens, *Membership Manager*

Memberships are valid for one year from date of application.

Make checks payable to the Ringling Museum Foundation, Inc.

Membership Categories:

Annual General Membership
❑ **$30 Individual**
Admits one

❑ **$50 Dual/Family**
Admits two
3 Guest passes

Annual Major Memberships
❑ **$100 Contributing**
Preview receptions
10 Guest passes

Name _____

Address _____

City _____ State ____ Zip _____ Phone _____

Payment method: ❑ Check   ❑ MasterCard   ❑ Visa

Amount: $ _____ Card #: _____ Expires: _____

Signature: _____

We also offer Sustaining ($250), Sponsoring ($500) and Colleague ($1,000) Memberships, all of which offer additional benefits. Please call the Membership Office for details at (941) 359-5748.

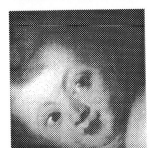

Rubens to Rhubarb

MAIL TO:

THE RINGLING MUSEUM FOUNDATION, INC.

Ringling Museum Shops

5401 Bay Shore Road, Sarasota, FL 34243

(941) 359-5732

ORDERED BY: Mr. Mrs. Ms. _____

Address _____

City _____

State _____ Zip _____

SHIP TO: Mr. Mrs. Ms. _____

Address _____

City _____

State _____ Zip _____

	Quantity	Price	Total Price
Rubens to Rhubarb		**$16.95**	$
Postal Charges	Merchandise Price		
1 copy $2.00	Members' 10% Discount		
2 copies $2.75	Florida Residents add Tax		
3 copies $3.50	Shipping *(see chart at left)*		
4 copies $4.25			
5 copies $5.00			
6 copies $5.75	**TOTAL ORDER**		$

METHOD OF PAYMENT

☐ Check/Money Order   ☐ Visa   ☐ MasterCard

Credit Card #_____ Exp. Date_____

Signature _____

THANK YOU!

Your purchases support The John and Mable Ringling Museum of Art.

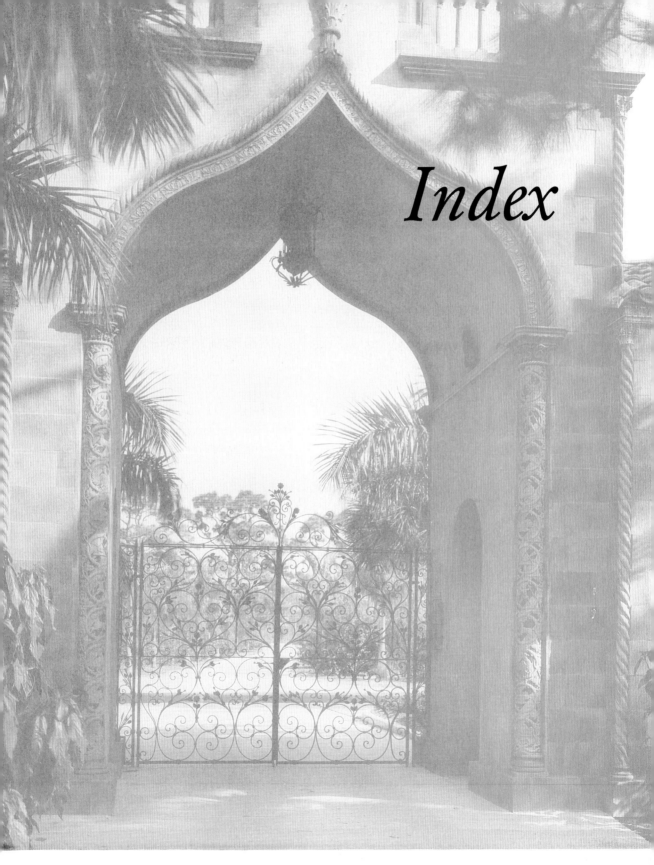

Index

Index

Index

Index

– W –

– Z –

Acknowledgments & Credits

The Historical Notes

A special acknowledgment goes to David C. Weeks who contributed the historical notes in this book. Dr. Weeks is an historian, an occasional lecturer, and a docent at The John and Mable Ringling Museum of Art.

Dr. Weeks' background includes two formal careers in Washington, DC, one in government and one in education. His federal service included the Central Intelligence Agency, the Departments of Justice, Commerce and Health and Human Services. He was an adjunct professor at the American University Center for Technology and Administration and a research associate professor at George Washington University.

He was educated at McGill University and at the University of London where he received a Ph. D. in Diplomatic History. Dr. Weeks' publications include the book, *Ringling, the Florida Years, 1911-1936*. He currently resides in Bradenton, Florida.

—•••••—

The Section Divider Pages

Permission to use the 1931 photographs of the Cà d'Zan by photographer Samuel Gottscho is from The University of Syracuse, Syracuse, NY.

Page	Section Title	View
15	Appetizers & Dips	West view of the marble terrace and the Spanish barrelled tile roof.
37	Soups & Salads	Late 19th-century furniture in the entrance foyer.
63	Meat	View from the belvedere tower overlooking Sarasota Bay.
85	Poultry & Seafood	Spanish-style wrought-iron standing lamps flank a lunette mural.
115	Vegetables	Southwest doors with hand-blown, tinted, stained-glass windows.
129	Pasta, Grains & Bread	The solid oak table and green-glazed chairs in the Breakfast Room.
151	Desserts	Belvedere tower with decorative terra cotta tile designs.
167	Pies & Cakes	Ornate glazed terra cotta tiles adorn the tower.
191	Cookies & Candy	Interior of the main entrance flanked by Flemish tapestries.
217	Healthy Substitutes & Seasonings	The balcony of John Ringling's bedroom.
225	Index	Gatehouse to Cà d'Zan, decorated with Masonic symbols.

On the Covers

The front cover is a detail of Jan Davidsz. de Heem, Dutch, (1606 - 1683/84), ***Still Life with Parrots***, late 1640s, oil on canvas. The John and Mable Ringling Museum of Art.

The back cover photograph is the Courtyard of The John and Mable Ringling Museum of Art, Sarasota, Florida, taken by Terry Shank.

Interior Color Photographs

Photographs of the Gateway to the Cà d'Zan (page 34), the statue of *David* in the Courtyard (page 36), the Rubens Gallery (page 70), and the Astor Gallery (page 72), by Terry Shank.

Permission to use the photograph of the Dining Room in the Cà d'Zan (page 138) from *Southern Accents*, Birmingham, AL.

Permission to use the photograph of the Museum Courtyard (page 139) from C. Harrison Conroy Co., Inc., Charlotte, NC.

Permission to use the photograph of The Ringling Bros. Poster (page 173) COURTESY OF RINGLING BROS. – BARNUM & BAILEY COMBINED SHOWS, INC. RINGLING BROS. is a trademark and service mark of Ringling Bros. – Barnum & Bailey Combined Shows, Inc.

All other photographs are from The John and Mable Ringling Museum of Art.

Notes